DAD,

I'm [so glad ...]
I do thank God that [He's] given
me the best dad there is. (Besides Him)

This is a book that I know
will help you - they are prayers
and other important things.

So - I hope that you'll
find it encouraging.

I Love You,
Jenny ☺

P.S. There's a devotion

Prayers That Avail Much
For Fathers

Prayers That Avail Much
For Fathers

James 5:16

Father's Edition

by
Word Ministries, Inc.

And this is the confidence that we have in him, that, if we ask any thing according to his will, he heareth us: and if we know that he hear us, whatsoever we ask, we know that we have the petitions that we desired of him.

1 John 5:14,15

Harrison House
Tulsa, Oklahoma

Unless otherwise indicated, all Scripture quotations are taken from the *King James Version* of the Bible.

Some Scripture quotations marked AMP are taken from *The Amplified Bible, New Testament*. Copyright © 1954, 1958 by The Lockman Foundation, La Habra, California. Used by permission.

Some Scripture quotations marked AMP are taken from *The Amplified Bible, Old Testament*. Copyright © 1962, 1964 by Zondervan Publishing House, Grand Rapids, Michigan. Used by permission.

Prayers and confessions are paraphrased from these versions unless otherwise stated.

Prayers That Avail Much
For Fathers
ISBN 0-89274-955-5
Copyright © 1990, 1994 by Word Ministries, Inc.
P. O. Box 76532
Atlanta, Georgia 30358

Published by Harrison House, Inc.
P. O. Box 35035
Tulsa, Oklahoma 74153

Printed in the United States of America. All rights reserved under International Copyright Law. Contents and/or cover may not be reproduced in whole or in part in any form without the express written consent of the Publisher.

Presented to

DAD

By

JENNY

Date

12/25/94

Occasion

Christmas & Encouragement

Marriage

For this cause shall a man leave father and mother, and shall cleave to his wife: and they twain shall be one flesh.
Matthew 19:5

Mr. **Warren Stewart**

was married to

Miss **Pam Hyden**

Date **Nov. 83**

Births

Lo children are an heritage of the Lord: and the fruit of the womb is His reward.
Psalm 127:3

Jennifer
Becky
John
Andrew

Contents

Foreword	11
Preface	15
Introduction	19
Personal Confessions	29

Part I — Prayers That Avail Much

Prayers for Personal Concerns

1	The Children	33
2	The Home	35
3	Harmonious Marriage	37
4	Compatibility in Marriage	38
5	The Setting of Proper Priorities	40
6	Godly Wisdom in the Affairs of Life	42
7	Strength To Overcome Cares and Burdens	44
8	Renewing the Mind	46
9	Conquering the Thought Life	48
10	Boldness	50

Prayers of Commitment

11	To Walk in God's Wisdom and His Perfect Will	52
12	To Walk in the Word	54
13	To Put on the Armor of God	56
14	To Bear Fruit	58
15	To Help Others	60
16	To Walk in Love	62
17	To Walk in Forgiveness	64
18	To Live Free From Worry	66
19	To Receive Jesus as Saviour and Lord	68
20	To Receive the Infilling of the Holy Spirit	69

Prayers for Finances

21	Prosperity	70
22	Dedication of Your Tithes	72
23	Being Equipped for Success	73

Prayers for God's People
- 24 The Body of Christ — 75
- 25 Ministers — 77
- 26 Church Teachers — 79
- 27 Missionaries — 81
- 28 Success of a Meeting — 83
- 29 Vision for a Church — 85
- 30 Revival — 87
- 31 Unity and Harmony — 89
- 32 Personal Prayer of a Pastor for the Congregation — 91

Prayers for the World
- 33 Salvation of the Lost — 93
- 34 Nations and Continents — 95
- 35 Protection From Terrorism — 100
- 36 Protection and Deliverance of a City — 102

Prayers for Those in Authority
- 37 American Government — 105
- 38 School Systems and Children — 107

Prayers to the Father
- 39 Adoration — 110
- 40 Divine Intervention — 113
- 41 Submission — 115
- 42 Provision — 117
- 43 Forgiveness — 119
- 44 Guidance and Deliverance — 121
- 45 Praise — 122

Prayers for Victory
- 46 Victory Over Pride — 124
- 47 Victory Over Fear — 125
- 48 Victory Over Depression — 127
- 49 Victory Over Gluttony — 129
- 50 Victory in Court Cases — 131

Part II — What the Word Says

What the Word Says About You
- Being a Father Who Is Godly — 135
- Being a Father Who Is Loving — 137
- Being a Father Who Is Giving — 139
- Being a Father Who Listens — 141
- Being a Father Who Is Patient — 143
- Being a Father Who Is Knowledgeable — 145
- Being a Father Who Is Honorable — 147
- Being a Father Who Is a Leader — 149
- Being a Father Who Is Faithful — 151
- Being a Father Who Is Kind — 153
- If You Need Wisdom — 155
- If You Have Difficulty Being the Spiritual Leader in Your Home — 157
- If You Need to Make a Major Career Decision — 159
- If You Need Peace Within — 161
- If You Need To Forgive — 163
- If You Need To Overcome Anger — 165
- If You Need Motivation — 167
- If Your Job Is Unsatisfying — 169
- If You Feel Like a Failure — 171
- If You Are Facing Sexual Temptation — 173

What the Word Says About You and Your Family
- If Your Wife Is Unsupportive of Your Dreams and Goals — 175
- If Your Wife Has Responsibilities out of the Home — 177
- If Your Daily Family Devotions Seem Difficult — 179
- If Your Child Is Rebellious Toward You — 181
- If Your Child Is Rebellious Toward God — 183
- If Your Child Is Withdrawing From You — 185
- If Your Child Encounters Peer Pressure — 187
- If Your Child Has a Poor Self-Image — 189
- If Your Child Is Sick — 191

Part III — The Family Man
"The Making of a Family"
    by Richard Exley   195

Part IV — Getting Into the Word
31-Day Devotional by Dick Mills   209
Reading the Bible in One Year   247
Bibliography

Foreword

This special *Prayers That Avail Much, for Fathers* was created and designed for you, because you are important to your family and your Heavenly Father. The unique features in this book will strengthen you spiritually, physically and emotionally and are designed for your daily use as you seek to become a more godly and Spirit-led father.

Because of the great upheaval the family has undergone in recent years, men must learn to lead their families with a stronger, more godly conviction than ever before. Fathers are often forgotten family members as they pursue career goals and leave the parenting to their wives. But God has called each man to be the head of his house, to be the covering for all the members of his family. For this reason, we have published *Prayers That Avail much, for Fathers*; we want to encourage and exhort you with God's Word.

We have included different sections within this book to help you in each area of your life. Here is a brief description and a guide to using these sections.

The prayers in Part I are taken from *Prayers That Avail Much, Volumes I and II*, and are based upon God's Word. Fifty prayers help you pray more effectively by praying the Scripture. These prayers were written for specific situations that fathers face and have special meaning for you. Use these scriputrally based prayers during your daily quiet time as a solid Bible reference. You will find encouragement and strength in praying God's Word over your life and family.

Part II is devoted completely to the promises that God's Word holds for you as a father. Appropriately titled "What the Word Says," there are more than five hundred scriptures covering situations and phases of life that fathers experience. Use these scriptures for encouragement and godly guidance. These are grouped into two sections, "What the Word Says About You," and "What the Word Says About You and Your Family." The Bible holds promises specifically for fathers, and you can make these promises a reality in your life by applying these scriptures.

God has established the man to be the head of the household, but divorce and other factors in society have left many men without the know-how to actually be loving and effective leaders in their homes. Part III, "The Family Man," is a special section written by Richard Exley that gives some clear insights and scriptural foundations for men assuming the role of leader in the home. This excerpt from *Building Relationships That Last, Life's Bottom Line* also demonstrates the importance of family life to the growth and development of children. "The Making of a Family" is a powerful and inspiring teaching on how important fathers are in the family.

Part IV, "Getting Into the Word," gives you step-by-step, practical ways to study and apply God's Word. To help you develop a consistent and effective prayer life and study time, we have included a 31-Day Devotional and a Bible reading program.

The 31-Day Devotional by Dick Mills gives you a pattern for successful Bible study and daily encouragement from the Word of God and shows you how you can apply the Word each day. You will learn how to practice what the Bible teaches and grow spiritually because of your diligence in this special time with the Father.

The section called "Reading the Bible in One Year" gives you specific books and chapters of the of the Bible for you to read each day, including a daily passage from either the Psalms or Proverbs. As you read through the greatest

Book of all time, you will be encouraged, strengthened and loved by your Heavenly Father. As you seek to be closer to Him, He will draw closer to you.

What society demands from men is impossible without the help of God and a stable, consistent relationship with Jesus Christ. We have developed this book to encourage and assist you in strengthening your one-on-one relationship with Him. You, as a father, touch more people than you can imagine. A man cannot rely upon his own resources and inner strength to succeed; he needs godly strength. That is what we want *Prayers That Avail Much, for Fathers* to be to you — godly strength for being a man. May God bless you!

Preface

The prayers in this book are to be used by you for yourself and for others. They are a matter of the heart. Deliberately feed them into your spirit. Allow the Holy Spirit to make the Word a reality in your heart. Your spirit will become quickened to God's Word, and you will begin to think like God thinks and talk like He talks. You will find yourself poring over His Word — hungering for more and more. The Father rewards those who diligently seek Him. (Heb. 11:6.)

Meditate upon the Scriptures listed with these prayers. These are by no means the only Scriptures on certain subjects, but they are a beginning.

These prayers are to be a help and a guide to you in order for you to get better acquainted with your heavenly Father and His Word. Not only does His Word affect your life, but also it will affect your family and others through you, for you will be able to counsel accurately those who come to you for advice. If you cannot counsel someone with the Word, you do not have anything with which to counsel. Walk in God's counsel, and prize His wisdom. (Ps. 1; Prov. 4:7,8.) People are looking for something on which they can depend. When someone in need comes to you, you can point him to that portion in God's Word that is the answer to his problem. You become victorious, trustworthy, and the one with the answer, for your heart is fixed and established on His Word. (Ps. 112.)

Once you begin delving into God's Word, you must commit to ordering your conversation aright. (Ps. 50:23.) That is being a doer of the Word. Faith always has a good report. You cannot pray effectively for yourself, for someone else, or about something and then talk negatively about the matter. (Matt. 12:34-37.) This is being double-minded, and a double-minded man receives *nothing* from God. (James 1:6-8.)

In Ephesians 4:29-30 AMP it is written:

Let no foul or polluting language, nor evil word, nor unwholesome or worthless talk [ever] come out of your mouth; but only such [speech] as is good and beneficial to the spiritual progress of others, as is fitting to the need and the occasion, that it may be a blessing and give grace (God's favor) to those who hear it.

And do not grieve the Holy Spirit of God, (do not offend, or vex, or sadden Him) by whom you were sealed (marked, branded as God's own, secured) for the day of redemption — of final deliverance through Christ from evil and the consequences of sin.

Allow these words to sink into your innermost being. Our Father has much, so very much, to say about that little member, the tongue. (James 3.) Give the devil no opportunity by getting into worry, unforgiveness, strife, and criticism. Put a stop to idle and foolish talking. (Eph. 4:27; 5:4.) You are to be a blessing to others. (Gal. 6:10.)

Talk the answer, not the problem. The answer is in God's Word. You must have knowledge of that Word — revelation knowledge. (1 Cor. 2:7-16.)

As an intercessor, unite with others in prayer. United prayer is a mighty weapon that the Body of Christ is to use.

Believe you receive when you pray. Confess the Word. Hold fast to your confession of faith in God's Word. Allow your spirit to pray by the Holy Spirit. Praise God for the victory now before any manifestation. *Walk by faith and not by sight.* (2 Cor. 5:7.)

Don't be moved by adverse circumstances. As Satan attempts to challenge you, resist him steadfast in the faith — letting patience have her perfect work. (James 1:4.) Take the Sword of the Spirit and the shield of faith and quench his every fiery dart. (Eph. 6:16,17.) The entire substitutionary work of Christ was for you. Satan is now a defeated foe because Jesus conquered him. (Col. 2:14,15.) Satan is overcome by the blood of the Lamb and the Word of our testimony. (Rev. 12:11.) Fight the good fight of faith. (1 Tim. 6:12.) Withstand the adversary and be firm in faith against his onset — rooted, established, strong, and determined. (1 Pet. 5:9.) Speak God's Word boldly and courageously.

Your desire should be to please and to bless the Father. As you pray in line with His Word, He joyfully hears that you — His child — are living and walking in the Truth. (3 John 4.)

How exciting to know that the prayers of the saints are forever in the throne room. (Rev. 5:8.) Hallelujah!

Praise God for His Word and the limitlessness of prayer in the name of Jesus. It belongs to every child of God. Therefore, run with patience the race that is set before you, looking unto Jesus the author and finisher of your faith. (Heb. 12:1,2.) God's Word is able to build you up and give you your rightful inheritance among all God's set apart ones. (Acts 20:32.)

Commit yourself to pray and to pray correctly by approaching the throne with your mouth filled with His Word!

Introduction

> ... The earnest (heart-felt, continued) prayer of a righteous man makes tremendous power available — dynamic in its working.
>
> James 5:16 AMP

Prayer is fellowshiping with the Father — a vital, personal contact with God Who is more than enough. We are to be in constant communion with Him:

> For the eyes of the Lord are upon the righteous — those who are upright and in right standing with God — and His ears are attentive (open) to their prayer....
>
> 1 Peter 3:12 AMP

Prayer is not to be a religious form with no power. It is to be effective and accurate and bring *results.* God watches over His Words to perform it. (Jer. 1:12.)

Prayer that brings results must be based on God's Word.

> For the Word that God speaks is alive and full of power — making it active, operative, energizing and effective; it is sharper than any two-edged sword, penetrating to the dividing line of the breath of life (soul) and [the immortal] spirit, and of joints and marrow [that is, of the deepest parts of our nature] exposing and sifting and analyzing and judging the very thoughts and purposes of the heart.
>
> Hebrews 4:12 AMP

Prayer is the "living" Word in our mouths. Our mouths must speak forth faith, for faith is what pleases God. (Heb. 11:6.) We hold His Word up to Him in prayer, and our Father sees Himself in His Word.

God's Word is our contact with Him. We put Him in remembrance of His Word (Is. 43:26) placing a demand on His ability in the name of our Lord Jesus. We remind Him that He supplies all of our needs according to His riches in glory by Christ Jesus. (Phil. 4:19.) That Word does not return to Him void — without producing any effect, useless — but it *shall* accomplish that which He pleases and purposes, and it shall prosper in the thing for which He sent it. (Is. 55:11.) Hallelujah!

God did *not* leave us without His thoughts and His ways for we have His Word — His bond. God instructs us to call Him, and He will answer and show us great and mighty things. (Jer. 33:3.) Prayer is to be exciting — not drudgery.

It takes someone to pray. God moves as we pray in faith — believing. He says that His eyes run to and fro throughout the whole earth to show Himself strong in behalf of those whose hearts are blameless toward Him. (2 Chron. 16:9.) We are blameless. (Eph. 1:4.) We are His very own children. (Eph. 1:5.) We are His righteousness in Christ Jesus. (2 Cor. 5:21.) He tells us to come boldly to the throne of grace and *obtain* mercy and find grace to help in time of need — appropriate and well-timed help. (Heb. 4:16.) Praise the Lord!

The prayer armor is for every believer, every member of the Body of Christ, who will put it on and walk in it, for the weapons of our warfare are *not carnal* but mighty through God for the pulling down of the strongholds of the enemy (Satan, the god of this world, and all his demonic forces). Spiritual warfare takes place in prayer. (2 Cor. 10:4, Eph. 6:12,18.)

There are many different kinds of prayer, such as the prayer of thanksgiving and praise, the prayer of dedication and worship, and the prayer that changes *things* (not God). All prayer involves time of fellowshiping with the Father.

In Ephesians 6, we are instructed to take the Sword of the Spirit which is the Word of God and **pray at all times — on every occasion, in every season — in the Spirit, with all [manner of] prayer and entreaty** (Eph. 6:18 AMP).

In 1 Timothy 2 we are admonished and urged that **petitions, prayers, intercessions and thanksgivings be offered on behalf of all men** (1 Tim. 2:1 AMP). *Prayer is our responsibility.*

Prayer must be the foundation of every Christian endeavor. Any failure is a prayer failure. We are *not* to be ignorant concerning God's Word. God desires for His people to be successful, to be filled with a full, deep, and clear knowledge of His will (His Word), and to bear fruit in every good work. (Col. 1:9-13.) We then bring honor and glory to Him. (John 15:8.) He desires that we know how to pray for **the prayer of the upright is his delight** (Prov. 15:8).

Our Father has not left us helpless. Not only has He given us His Word, but also He has given us the Holy Spirit to help our infirmities when we know not how to pray as we ought. (Rom. 8:26.) Praise God! Our Father has provided His people with every possible avenue to insure their complete and total victory in this life in the name of our Lord Jesus. (1 John 5:3-5.)

We pray to the Father, in the name of Jesus, through the Holy Spirit, according to the Word!

Using God's Word on purpose, specifically, in prayer is one means of prayer, and it is a most effective and accurate means. Jesus said, **The words (truths) that I have been speaking to you are spirit and life** (John 6:63 AMP).

When Jesus faced Satan in the wilderness, He said, "It is written. . . it is written. . . it is written." We are to live, be upheld, and sustained by every Word that proceeds from the mouth of God. (Matt. 4:4.)

James, by the Spirit, admonishes that we do not have, because we do not ask. We ask and receive not, because we ask amiss. (James 4:2,3.) We must heed that admonishment now for we are to become experts in prayer rightly dividing the Word of Truth. (2 Tim. 2:15.)

Using the Word in prayer is *not* taking it out of context, for His Word in us is the key to answered prayer — to prayer that brings results. He is able to do exceedingly abundantly above all we ask or think, according to the power that works in us. (Eph. 3:20.) The power lies within God's Word. It is anointed by the Holy Spirit. The Spirit of God does not lead us apart from the Word, for the Word is of the Spirit of God. We apply that Word personally to ourselves and to others — not adding to or taking from it — in the name of Jesus. We apply the Word to the *now* — to those things, circumstances, and situations facing each of us *now*.

Paul was very specific and definite in his praying. The first chapters of Ephesians, Philippians, Colossians, and 2 Thessalonians are examples of how Paul prayed for believers. There are numerous others. *Search them out.* Paul wrote under the inspiration of the Holy Spirit. We can use these Spirit-given prayers today!

In 2 Corinthians 1:11, 2 Corinthians 9:14, and Philippians 1:4, we see examples of how believers prayed one for another — putting others first in their life with *joy.* Our faith does work by love. (Gal. 5:6.) We grow spiritually as we reach out to help others — praying for and with them and holding out to them the Word of Life. (Phil. 2:16.)

Man is a spirit, he has a soul, and he lives in a body. (1 Thess. 5:23.) In order to operate successfully, each of these three parts must be fed properly. The soul or intellect feeds on intellectual food to produce intellectual strength. The body feeds on physical food to produce physical strength. The spirit — the heart or inward man

— is the real you, the part that has been reborn in Christ Jesus. It must feed on spirit food which is God's Word in order to produce and develop faith. As we feast upon God's Word, our minds become renewed with His Word, and we have a fresh mental and spiritual attitude. (Eph. 4:23,24.)

Likewise, we are to present our bodies a living sacrifice, holy, acceptable unto God (Rom. 12:1) and not let that body dominate us but bring it into subjection to the spirit man. (1 Cor. 9:27.) God's Word is healing and health to all our flesh. (Prov. 4:22.) Therefore, God's Word affects each part of us — spirit, soul and body. We become vitally united to the Father, to Jesus, and to the Holy Spirit — one with Them. (John 16:13-15, John 17:21, Col. 2:10.)

God's Word, this spirit food, takes root in our hearts, is formed by the tongue, and is spoken out of our mouths. This is creative power. The spoken Word works as we confess it and then apply the action to it.

Be doers of the Word, and not hearers only, deceiving your own selves. (James 1:22.) Faith without works or corresponding action is *dead*. (James 2:17.) Don't be mental assenters — those who agree that the Bible is true but never act on it. *Real faith is acting on God's Word now.* We cannot build faith without practicing the Word. We cannot develop an effective prayer life that is anything but empty words unless God's Word actually has a part in our lives. We are to hold fast to our *confession* of the Word's truthfulness. Our Lord Jesus is the High Priest of our confession (Heb. 3:1), and He is the Guarantee of a better agreement — a more excellent and advantageous covenant. (Heb. 7:22.)

Prayer does not cause faith to work, but faith causes prayer to work. Therefore, any prayer problem is a problem of doubt — doubting the integrity of the Word and the ability of God to stand behind His promises or the statements of fact in the Word.

We can spend fruitless hours in prayer if our hearts are not prepared beforehand. Preparation of the heart, the spirit, comes from meditation in the Father's Word, meditation on what we are in Christ, what He is to us, and what the Holy Spirit can mean to us as we become God-inside minded. As God told Joshua (Josh. 1:8), as we meditate on the Word day and night, and do according to all that is written, then shall we make our way prosperous and have good success. We are to attend to God's Word, submit to His sayings, keep them in the center of our hearts, and put away contrary talk. (Prov. 4:20-24.)

When we use God's Word in prayer, this is *not* something we just rush through uttering once, and we are finished. Do *not* be mistaken. There is nothing "magical" nor "manipulative" about it — no set pattern or device in order to satisfy what we want or think out of our flesh. Instead we are holding God's Word before Him. We confess what He says belongs to us.

We expect His divine intervention while we choose not to look at the things that are seen but at the things that are unseen, for the things that are seen are subject to change. (2 Cor. 4:18.)

Prayer based upon the Word rises above the senses, contacts the Author of the Word and sets His spiritual laws into motion. It is not just saying prayers that gets results, but it is spending time with the Father, learning His wisdom, drawing on His strength, being filled with His quietness, and basking in His love that bring results to our prayers. Praise the Lord!

* * *

The prayers in this book are designed to teach and train you in the art of personal confession and intercessory prayer. As you pray them, you will be reinforcing the prayer armor which we have been instructed to put on in

Ephesians 6:11. The fabric from which the armor is made is the Word of God. We are to live by every word that proceeds from the mouth of God.

We desire the whole counsel of God, because we know it changes us. By receiving that counsel, you will be ... **transformed (changed) by the [entire] renewal of your mind — by its new ideals and attitude — so that you may prove [for yourselves] what is the good and acceptable and perfect will of God, even the thing which is good and acceptable and perfect [in his sight for you]** (Rom. 12:2 AMP).

The prayers of personal confession of the Word of God for yourself can also be used as intercessory prayers for others by simply praying them in the third person, changing the pronouns *I* or *we* to the name of the person or persons for whom you are interceding and adjusting the verbs accordingly.

The prayers of intercession have blanks in which you are to fill in the spaces with the name of the person(s) for whom you are praying. These prayers of intercession can likewise be made into prayers of personal confession for yourself by inserting your own name and the proper personal pronoun in the appropriate places.

An often-asked question is: "How many times should I pray the same prayer?"

The answer is simple: you pray until you know that the answer is fixed in your heart. After that, you need to repeat the prayer whenever adverse circumstances or long delays cause you to be tempted to doubt that your prayer has been heard and your request granted.

The Word of God is your weapon against the temptation to lose heart and grow weary in your prayer life. When that Word of promise becomes fixed in your heart, you will find yourself praising, giving glory to God for the answer, even when the only evidence you have of that answer is your own faith.

Another question often asked is: "When we repeat prayers more than once, aren't we praying 'vain repetitions'?"

Obviously, such people are referring to the admonition of Jesus when He told His disciples: **And when you pray do not (multiply words, repeating the same ones over and over, and) heap up phrases as the Gentiles do, for they think they will be heard for their much speaking** (Matt. 6:7 AMP). Praying the Word of God is not praying the kind of prayer that the "heathen" pray. You will note in 1 Kings 18:25-29 the manner of prayer that was offered to the gods who could not hear. That is not the way you and I pray. The words that we speak are not vain, but they are spirit and life, and mighty through God to the pulling down of strongholds. We have a God Whose eyes are over the righteous and Whose ears are open to us: when we pray, He hears us.

You are the righteousness of God in Christ Jesus, and your prayers will avail much. They will bring salvation to the sinner, deliverance to the oppressed, healing to the sick, and prosperity to the poor. They will usher in the next move of God in the earth. In addition to affecting outward circumstances and other people, your prayers will also have an effect upon you. In the very process of praying, your life will be changed as you go from faith to faith and from glory to glory.

As a Christian, your first priority is to love the Lord your God with your entire being, and your neighbor as yourself. You are called to be an intercessor, a man or woman of prayer. You are to seek the face of the Lord as you inquire, listen, meditate and consider in the temple of the Lord.

As one of "God's set-apart ones," the will of the Lord for your life is the same as it is for the life of every other true believer: **. . . seek ye first the kingdom of God, and his righteousness; and all these things shall be added unto you** (Matt. 6:33).

Personal Confessions

Jesus is Lord over my spirit, my soul, and my body. (Phil. 2:9-11.)

Jesus has been made unto me wisdom, righteousness, sanctification, and redemption. I can do all things through Christ Who strengthens me. (1 Cor. 1:30, Phil. 4:13.)

The Lord is my shepherd. I do not want. My God supplies all my need according to His riches in glory in Christ Jesus. (Ps. 23, Phil. 4:19.)

I do not fret or have anxiety about anything. I do not have a care. (Phil. 4:6, 1 Pet. 5:6,7.)

I am the Body of Christ. I am redeemed from the curse, because Jesus bore my sicknesses and carried my diseases in His own body. By His stripes I am healed. I forbid any sickness or disease to operate in my body. Every organ, every tissue of my body functions in the perfection in which God created it to function. I honor God and bring glory to Him in my body. (Gal. 3:13, Matt. 8:17, 1 Pet. 2:24, 1 Cor. 6:20.)

I have the mind of Christ and hold the thoughts, feelings, and purposes of His heart. (1 Cor. 2:16.)

I am a believer and not a doubter. I hold fast to my confession of faith. I decide to walk by faith and practice faith. My faith comes by hearing and hearing by the Word of God. Jesus is the author and the developer of my faith. (Heb. 4:14, Heb. 11:6, Rom. 10:17, Heb. 12:2.)

The love of God has been shed abroad in my heart by the Holy Spirit and His love abides in me richly. I keep myself in the Kingdom of light, in love, in the Word, and the wicked one touches me not. (Rom. 5:5, 1 John 4:16, 1 John 5:18.)

I tread upon serpents and scorpions and over all the power of the enemy. I take my shield of faith and quench his every fiery dart. Greater is He Who is in me than he who is in the world. (Ps. 91:13, Eph. 6:16, 1 John 4:4.)

I am delivered from this present evil world. I am seated with Christ in heavenly places. I reside in the Kingdom of God's dear Son. The law of the Spirit of life in Christ Jesus has made me free from the law of sin and death. (Gal. 1:4, Eph. 2:6, Col. 1:13, Rom. 8:2.)

I fear *not* for God has given me a spirit of power, of love, and of a sound mind. God is on my side. (2 Tim. 1:7, Rom. 8:31.)

I hear the voice of the Good Shepherd. I hear my Father's voice, and the voice of a stranger I will not follow. I roll my works upon the Lord. I commit and trust them wholly to Him. He will cause my thoughts to become agreeable to His will, and so shall my plans be established and succeed. (John 10:27, Prov. 16:3.)

I am a world overcomer because I am born of God. I represent the Father and Jesus well. I am a useful member in the Body of Christ. I am His workmanship recreated in Christ Jesus. My Father God is all the while effectually at work in me both to will and do His good pleasure. (1 John 5:4-5, Eph. 2:10, Phil. 2:13.)

I let the Word dwell in me richly. He Who began a good work in me will continue until the day of Christ. (Col. 3:16, Phil. 1:6.)

Part I
Prayers That Avail Much

1
The Children

Father, in the name of Jesus, I pray and confess Your Word over my children and surround them with my faith — faith in Your Word that You watch over it to perform it! I confess and believe that my children are disciples of Christ taught of the Lord and obedient to Your will. Great is the peace and undisturbed composure of my children, because You, God, contend with that which contends with my children, and You give them safety and ease them.

Father, You will perfect that which concerns me. *I commit and cast the care of my children once and for all over on You, Father.* They are in Your hands, and I am positively persuaded that You are able to guard and keep that which I have committed to You. You are more than enough!

I confess that my children obey their parents in the Lord as His representatives, because this is just and right. My children _____ honor, esteem, and value as precious their parents; for this is the first commandment with a promise: that all may be well with my children and that they may live long on earth. I believe and confess that my children choose life and love You, Lord, obey Your voice, and cling to You; for You are their life and the length of their days. Therefore, my children are the head and not the tail, and shall be above only and not beneath. They are blessed when they come in and when they go out.

I believe and confess that You give Your angels charge over my children to accompany and defend and preserve them in all their ways. You, Lord, are their refuge and fortress. You are their glory and the lifter of their heads.

As parents, we will not provoke, irritate, or fret our children. We will not be hard on them or harass them, or cause them to become discouraged, sullen, or morose, or feel inferior and frustrated. We will not break or wound their spirits, but we will rear them tenderly in the training, discipline, counsel, and admonition of the Lord. We will train them in the way they should go, and when they are old they will not depart from it.

O Lord, my Lord, how excellent (majestic and glorious) is Your name in all the earth! You have set Your glory on or above the heavens. Out of the mouth of babes and unweaned infants You have established strength because of Your foes, that You might silence the enemy and the avenger. I sing praise to Your name, O Most High. *The enemy is turned back from my children in the name of Jesus!* They increase in wisdom and in favor with God and man.

Scripture References

Jeremiah 1:12	Psalm 91:11
Isaiah 54:13	Psalm 91:2
Isaiah 49:25	Psalm 3:3
1 Peter 5:7	Colossians 3:21
2 Timothy 1:12	Ephesians 6:4
Ephesians 6:1-3	Proverbs 22:6
Deuteronomy 30:19,20	Psalm 8:1,2
Deuteronomy 28:13	Psalm 9:2,3
Deuteronomy 28:3,6	Luke 2:52

2
The Home

Father, I thank You that You have blessed me with all spiritual blessings in Christ Jesus.

Through skillful and godly wisdom is my house (my life, my home, my family) built, and by understanding it is established on a sound and good foundation. And by knowledge shall the chambers (of its every area) be filled with all precious and pleasant riches — great priceless treasure. The house of the uncompromisingly righteous shall stand. Prosperity and welfare are in my house in the name of Jesus.

My house is securely built. It is founded on a rock — revelation knowledge of Your Word, Father. Jesus is my Cornerstone. Jesus is Lord of my household. Jesus is our Lord — spirit, soul, and body.

Whatever may be our task, we work at it heartily as something done for You, Lord, and not for men. We love each other with the God kind of love, and we dwell in peace. My home is deposited into Your charge, entrusted to Your protection and care.

Father, as for me and my house we shall serve the Lord in Jesus' name. Hallelujah!

Prayers for Personal Concerns

Scripture References

Ephesians 1:3
Proverbs 24:3,4 AMP
Proverbs 15:6
Proverbs 12:7 AMP
Psalm 112:3
Luke 6:48
Acts 4:11

Acts 16:31
Philippians 2:10,11
Colossians 3:23
Colossians 3:14,15
Acts 20:32
Joshua 24:15

3
Harmonious Marriage

Father, in the name of Jesus, it is written in Your Word that love is shed abroad in our hearts by the Holy Ghost Who is given to us. Because You are in us, we acknowledge that love reigns supreme. We believe that love is displayed in full expression enfolding and knitting us together in truth, making us perfect for every good work to do Your will, working in us that which is pleasing in Your sight.

We live and conduct ourselves and our marriage honorably and becomingly. We esteem it as precious, worthy, and of great price. *We commit ourselves to live in mutual harmony and accord with one another* delighting in each other, being of the same mind and united in spirit.

Father, we believe and say that we are gentle, compassionate, courteous, tender-hearted, and humble-minded. We seek peace, and it keeps our hearts in quietness and assurance. Because we follow after love and dwell in peace, our prayers are not hindered in any way, in the name of Jesus. We are heirs together of the grace of God.

Our marriage grows stronger day by day in the bond of unity because it is founded on Your Word and rooted and grounded in Your love. Father, we thank You for the performance of it, in Jesus' name.

Scripture References

Romans 5:5	Ephesians 4:32
Philippians 1:9	Isaiah 32:17
Colossians 3:14	Philippians 4:7
Colossians 1:10	1 Peter 3:7
Philippians 2:13	Ephesians 3:17,18
Philippians 2:2	Jeremiah 1:12

4
Compatibility in Marriage

Father, in the name of Jesus, I pray and confess that my spouse and I endure long and are patient and kind; that we are never envious and never boil over with jealousy. We are not boastful or vainglorious, and we do not display ourselves haughtily. We are not conceited or arrogant and inflated with pride.

We are not rude and unmannerly, and we do not act unbecomingly. We do not insist on our own rights or our own way, for we are not self-seeking or touchy or fretful or resentful.

We take no account of the evil done to us and pay no attention to a suffered wrong. We do not rejoice at injustice and unrighteousness, but we rejoice when right and truth prevail.

We bear up under anything and everything that comes. We are ever ready to believe the best of each other. Our hopes are fadeless under all circumstances. We endure everything without weakening. *Our love never fails* — it never fades out or becomes obsolete or comes to an end.

We are confessing that our lives and our family's lives lovingly express truth in all things that we speak truly, deal truly, and live truly. We are enfolded in love and have grown up in every way and in all things. We esteem and delight in one another, forgiving one another readily and freely as God in Christ has forgiven us. We are imitators of God and copy His example as well-beloved children imitate their father.

Compatibility in Marriage

Thank You, Father, that our marriage grows stronger each day because it is founded on Your Word and on Your kind of love. We give You the praise for it all, Father, in the name of Jesus.

Scripture Reference

1 Corinthians 13:4-8 AMP	Ephesians 4:15,32
1 Corinthians 14:1	Ephesians 5:1,2

5
The Setting of Proper Priorities

Father, in the name of Jesus, I come before You. Spirit of Truth, Who comes from the Father, it is You Who guides me into all truth. According to 3 John 2 it is God's will that I prosper in every way and that my body keeps well, even as my soul keeps well and prospers.

One thing I ask of You, Lord, one thing will I seek after, inquire for and [insistently] require, that I may dwell in Your house [in Your presence], all the days of my life, to behold and gaze upon Your beauty. I come to meditate, consider and inquire in Your temple (*about success in life*).

Father, You have said, **I will not in any way fail you nor give you up nor leave you without support. [I will] not, [I will] not, [I will] not in any degree leave you helpless, nor forsake nor let [you] down, [relax my hold on you]. — Assuredly not** (Heb. 13:5 AMP)! So I take comfort and am encouraged and confidently and boldly say that the Lord is my Helper, I will not be seized with alarm — I will not fear or dread or be terrified. What can man do to me?

In the name of Jesus, I am strong and very courageous, that I may do according to all Your Word. I turn not from it to the right hand or to the left, that I may prosper wherever I go. The Word of God shall not depart out of my mouth, but I shall meditate on it day and night. I hear therefore and am watchful to keep the instructions, the laws and precepts of my Lord God, that it may be well with me and that I may increase exceedingly, as the Lord God has promised me, in a land flowing with milk and honey. The Lord my God is one Lord — the only Lord. And I shall love the Lord my

The Setting of Proper Priorities

God with all my [mind and] heart, and with my entire being, and with all my might. And I will love my neighbor as myself.

Jesus, You said that when I do this I will live — enjoy active, blessed, endless life in the Kingdom of God. Therefore, I will not worry or be anxious about what I am going to eat, or what I am going to have to drink, or what I am going to have to wear. My heavenly Father knows that I need them all. But I purpose in my heart to seek for (aim at and strive after) first of all Your Kingdom, Lord, and Your righteousness [Your way of doing and being right], and then all these things taken together will be given me besides.

Now thanks be to You, Father, Who always causes me to triumph in Christ!

Scripture References

John 16:13a	Deuteronomy 6:1,3-5 AMP
Psalm 27:4 AMP	Luke 19:27,28 AMP
Hebrews 13:5b,6 AMP	Matthew 6:31-33 AMP
Joshua 1:7,8a AMP	2 Corinthians 2:14

6
Godly Wisdom in the Affairs of Life

Father, You said if anyone lacks wisdom, let him ask of You, Who giveth to all men liberally, and upbraideth not; and it shall be given him. Therefore, I ask in faith, nothing wavering, to be filled with the knowledge of Your will in all wisdom and spiritual understanding. Today I incline my ear unto wisdom, and apply my heart to understanding so that I might receive that which has been freely given unto me.

In the name of Jesus, I receive skill and godly wisdom and instruction. I discern and comprehend the words of understanding and insight. I receive instruction in wise dealing and the discipline of wise thoughtfulness, righteousness, justice, and integrity.

Prudence, knowledge, discretion, and discernment are given to me. I increase in knowledge. As a person of understanding, I acquire skill and attain to sound counsels [so that I may be able to steer my course rightly].

Wisdom will keep, defend, and protect me; I love her and she guards me. I prize Wisdom highly and exalt her; she will bring me to honor because I embrace her. She gives to my head a wreath of gracefulness; a crown of beauty and glory will she deliver to me. Length of days is in her right hand, and in her left hand are riches and honor.

Jesus has been made unto me wisdom, and in Him are all the treasures of [divine] wisdom, [of comprehensive insight into the ways and purposes of God], and [all the

Godly Wisdom in the Affairs of Life

riches of spiritual] knowledge and enlightenment are stored up and lie hidden. God has hidden away sound and godly wisdom and stored it up for me, for I am the righteousness of God in Christ Jesus.

Therefore, I will walk in paths of uprightness. When I walk, my steps shall not be hampered — my path will be clear and open; and when I run I shall not stumble. I take fast hold of instruction, and do not let her go; I guard her, for she is my life. I let my eyes look right on [with fixed purpose], and my gaze is straight before me. I consider well the path of my feet, and I let all my ways be established and ordered aright.

Father, in the name of Jesus, I look carefully to how I walk! I live purposefully and worthily and accurately, not as unwise and witless, but as a wise — sensible, intelligent person; making the very most of my time — buying up every opportunity.

Scripture References

James 1:5,6a	1 Corinthians 1:30
Colossians 1:9b	Colossians 2:3 AMP
Proverbs 2:2	Proverbs 2:7 AMP
Proverbs 1:2-5 AMP	2 Corinthians 5:21
Proverbs 4:6,8,9 AMP	Proverbs 4:11-13,25,26 AMP
Proverbs 3:16 AMP	Ephesians 5:15,16 AMP

7
Strength To Overcome Cares and Burdens

Why are you cast down, O my inner self? And why should you moan over me and be disquieted within me?

Father, You set yourself against the proud and haughty, but give grace [continually] unto the humble. I submit myself therefore to You, God. In the name of Jesus, I resist the devil, and he will flee from me. I resist the cares of the church which try to pressure me daily. Except the Lord builds the house, they labor in vain who build it.

Jesus, I come to You, for I labor and am heavy-laden and over burdened, and You cause me to rest — You will ease and relieve and refresh my soul. I take Your yoke upon me, and I learn of You; for You are gentle (meek) and humble (lowly) in heart, and I will find rest — relief, ease and refreshment and recreation and blessed quiet — for my soul. For Your yoke is wholesome (*easy*) — not harsh, hard, sharp or pressing, but comfortable, gracious and pleasant; and Your burden is light and easy to be borne.

I cast my burden on You, Lord, [releasing the weight of it] and You will sustain me; I thank You that You will never allow me, the [consistently] righteous, to be moved — made to slip, fall or fail.

In the name of Jesus, I withstand the devil. I am firm in my faith [against his onset] — rooted, established, strong, immovable and determined. I cease from [the weariness and pain] of human labor; and am zealous and exert myself and strive diligently to enter into the rest [of God] — to know and experience it for myself.

Father, I thank You that Your presence goes with me, and that You give me rest. I am still and rest in You, Lord; I wait for You, and patiently stay myself upon You. I will not fret myself, nor shall I let my heart be troubled, neither shall I let it be afraid. I hope in You, God, and wait expectantly for You; for I shall yet praise You, for You are the help of my countenance, and my God.

Scripture References (AMP)

Psalm 42:11a
James 4:6,7
Psalm 127:1a
Matthew 11:28-30
Psalm 55:22
1 Peter 5:9a

Hebrews 4:10b,11
Exodus 33:14
Psalm 37:7
John 14:27b
Psalm 42:11b

8
Renewing the Mind

Father, I thank You that I shall prosper and be in health, even as my soul prospers. I have the mind of Christ, the Messiah, and do hold the thoughts (feelings and purposes) of His heart. I trust in You, Lord, with all my heart; I lean not unto my own understanding, but in all my ways I acknowledge You, and You shall direct my paths.

Today I submit myself to Your Word which exposes and sifts and analyzes and judges the very thoughts and purposes of my heart. (For the weapons of my warfare are not carnal, but mighty through You to the pulling down of strongholds — *intimidation, fears, doubts, unbelief and failure*.) I refute arguments and theories and reasonings and every proud and lofty thing that sets itself up against the (true) knowledge of God; and I lead every thought and purpose away captive into the obedience of Christ, the Messiah, the Anointed One.

Today I shall be transformed by the renewing of my mind, that I may prove what is that good and acceptable and perfect will of God. Your Word, Lord, shall not depart out of my mouth; but I shall meditate on it day and night, that I may observe to do according to all that is written therein: for then I shall make my way prosperous, then I shall have good success.

My thoughts are the thoughts of the diligent which tend only to plenteousness. Therefore I will not fret or have any anxiety about anything, but in everything by prayer and petition [definite requests] with thanksgiving continue to make my wants known unto You, Lord. And Your peace which transcends all understanding, shall garrison and mount guard over my heart and mind in Christ Jesus.

Today I fix my mind on whatever is *true*, whatever is *worthy* of *reverence* and is *honorable* and *seemly*, whatever is *just*, whatever is *pure*, whatever is *lovely* and *lovable*, whatever is *kind* and *winsome* and *gracious*. If there is any *virtue* and *excellence*, if there is anything *worthy* of *praise*, I will think on and weigh and take account of these things.

Today I roll my works upon You, Lord — I commit and trust them wholly to You; [You will cause my thoughts to become agreeable to Your will, and] so shall my plans be established and succeed.

Scripture References

3 John 2	Romans 12:2
1 Corinthians 2:16b AMP	Joshua 1:8
Proverbs 3:5,6	Proverbs 21:5a
Hebrews 4:12b AMP	Philippians 4:6-8 AMP
2 Corinthians 10:4	Proverbs 16:3 AMP
2 Corinthians 10:5 AMP	

9
Conquering the Thought Life

In the name of Jesus, I take authority over my thought life. Even though I walk (live) in the flesh, I am not carrying on my warfare according to the flesh and using mere human weapons. For the weapons of my warfare are not physical (weapons of flesh and blood), but they are mighty before God for the overthrow and destruction of strongholds. I refute arguments and theories and reasonings and every proud and lofty thing that sets itself up against the (true) knowledge of God; and I lead every thought and purpose away captive into the obedience of Christ, the Messiah, the Anointed One.

With my soul I will bless the Lord with every thought and purpose in life. My mind will not wander out of the presence of God. My life shall glorify the Father — *spirit, soul, and body*. I take no account of the evil done to me — I pay no attention to a suffered wrong. It holds no place in my thought life. I am ever ready to believe the best of every person. I gird up the loins of my mind, and I set my mind and keep it set on what is above — the higher things — not on the things that are on the earth.

Whatever is true, whatever is worthy of reverence and is honorable and seemly, whatever is just, whatever is pure, whatever is lovely and lovable, whatever is kind and winsome and gracious, if there is any virtue and excellence, if there is anything worthy of praise, I will think on and weigh and take account of these things — I will fix my mind on them.

Conquring the Thought Life

The carnal mind is no longer operative for I have the mind of Christ, the Messiah, and do hold the thoughts (feelings and purposes) of His heart. In the name of Jesus, I will practice what I have learned and received and heard and seen in Christ, and model my way of living on it, and the God of peace — of untroubled, undisturbed well-being — will be with me.

Scripture References (AMP)

2 Corinthians 10:3-5	Colossians 3:2
Psalm 103:1	Philippians 4:8
1 Corinthians 6:20	1 Corinthians 2:16
1 Corinthians 13:5b,7a	Philippians 4:9
1 Peter 1:13	

10
Boldness

Father, in the name of Jesus, I am of good courage, I pray that You grant to me that with all *boldness* I speak forth Your Word. I pray that freedom of utterance be given me that I may open my mouth to proclaim *boldly* the mystery of the good news of the Gospel — that I may declare it *boldly* as I ought to do.

Father, I believe I receive that *boldness* now in the name of Jesus. Therefore, I have *boldness* to enter into the Holy of Holies by the blood of Jesus.

Because of my faith in Him, I dare to have the *boldness* (courage and confidence) of free access — an unreserved approach to You with freedom and without fear. I can draw fearlessly and confidently and *boldly* near to Your throne of grace and receive mercy and find grace to help in good time for my every need.

I am *bold* to pray. I come to the throne of God with my petitions, and for others who do not know how to ascend to the throne.

I will be *bold* toward Satan, demons, evil spirits, sickness, disease, and poverty for Jesus is the Head of all rule and authority — of every angelic principality and power. Disarming those who were ranged against us, Jesus made a *bold* display and public example of them triumphing over them. I am *bold* to say, "Satan, you are a defeated foe, for my God and my Jesus reign!"

I take comfort and am encouraged and confidently and *boldly* say, "The Lord is my Helper, I will not be seized with alarm — I will not fear or dread or be terrified. What can man do to me?" I dare to proclaim the Word toward heaven, toward hell, and toward earth. I am *bold* as a lion for I have been made the righteousness of God in Christ Jesus. I am complete in Him! Praise the name of Jesus!

Scripture References

Psalm 27:14
Acts 4:29
Ephesians 6:19,20 AMP
Mark 11:23,24
Hebrews 10:19
Ephesians 3:12 AMP

Hebrews 4:16 AMP
Colossians 2:10,15 AMP
Hebrews 13:6 AMP
Proverbs 28:1
2 Corinthians 5:21

11
To Walk in God's Wisdom and His Perfect Will

Father, I thank you that the communication of my faith becomes effectual by acknowledging every good thing which is in me in Christ Jesus. I hear the voice of the Good Shepherd. I hear my Father's voice, and the voice of a stranger I will not follow.

Father, I believe in my heart and say with my mouth that *this day the will of God is done in my life*. I walk in a manner worthy of You Lord, fully pleasing to You and desiring to please You in all things, bearing fruit in every good work. Jesus has been made unto me wisdom. I single-mindedly walk in that wisdom expecting to know what to do in every situation and to be on *top* of every circumstance!

I roll my works upon You, Lord, and You make my thoughts agreeable to Your will, and so my plans are established and succeed. You direct my steps and make them sure. I understand and firmly grasp what the will of the Lord is for I am not vague, thoughtless, or foolish. I stand firm and mature in spiritual growth, convinced and fully assured in everything willed by God.

Father, You have destined and appointed me to come progressively to know Your will — that is to perceive, to recognize more strongly and clearly, and to become better and more intimately acquainted with Your will. I thank you, Father, for the Holy Spirit Who abides permanently in me and Who guides me into all the truth — the whole, full truth — and speaks whatever He hears from the Father and

To Walk in God's Wisdom and His Perfect Will

announces and declares to me the things that are to come. I have the mind of Christ and hold the thoughts, feelings, and purposes of His heart.

So, Father, I have entered into that blessed rest by adhering, trusting, and relying on You in the name of Jesus. Hallelujah!

Scripture References

Philemon 6	Ephesians 5:17
John 10:27	Colossians 4:12 AMP
John 10:5	Acts 22:14
Colossians 1:9,10 AMP	1 John 2:20,27
1 Corinthians 1:30	1 Corinthians 2:16
James 1:5-8	Hebrews 4:10
Proverbs 16:3,9 AMP	John 16:13 AMP

12
To Walk in the Word

Father, in the name of Jesus, *I commit myself to walk in the Word.* Your Word living in me produces Your life in this world. I recognize that Your Word is integrity itself — steadfast, sure, eternal — and I trust my life to its provisions.

You have sent your Word forth into my heart. I let it dwell in me richly in all wisdom. I meditate in it day and night so that I may diligently act on it. The Incorruptible Seed, the Living Word, the Word of Truth, is abiding in my spirit. That Seed is growing mightily in me now, producing Your nature, Your life. It is my counsel, my shield, my buckler, my powerful weapon in battle. The Word is a lamp to my feet and a light to my path. It makes my way plain before me. I do not stumble, for my steps are ordered in the Word.

The Holy Spirit leads and guides me into all the truth. He gives me understanding, discernment, and comprehension so that I am preserved from the snare of the evil one.

I delight myself in You and Your Word. Because of that, You put Your desires within my heart. I commit my way unto You, and You bring it to pass. I am confident that You are at work in me now both to will and to do all Your good pleasure.

I exalt Your Word, hold it in high esteem and give it first place. *I make my schedule around Your Word.* I make the Word final authority to settle all questions that confront me. I choose to agree with the Word of God, and I choose to disagree with any thoughts, conditions, or circumstances contrary to Your Word. I boldly and confidently say that my heart is fixed and established on the solid foundation — the living Word of God!

Scripture References

Hebrews 4:12	1 Peter 3:12
Colossians 3:16	Colossians 4:2
Joshua 1:8	Ephesians 6:10
1 Peter 1:23	Luke 18:1
Psalm 91:4	James 5:16
Psalm 119:105	Psalm 37:4,5
Psalm 37:23	Philippians 2:13
Colossians 1:9	2 Corinthians 10:5
John 16:13	Psalm 112:7,8

13
To Put on the Armor of God

In the name of Jesus, I put on the whole armor of God, that I may be able to stand against the wiles of the devil, for I wrestle not against flesh and blood, but against principalities, powers, the rulers of the darkness of this world, and against spiritual wickedness in high places.

Therefore I take unto myself the whole armor of God, that I may be able to withstand in the evil day, and having done all, to stand. I stand, therefore, having my loins girt about with truth. Your Word, Lord, which is truth, contains all the weapons of my warfare which are not carnal, but mighty through God to the pulling down of strongholds.

I have on the breastplate of righteousness; which is faith and love. My feet are shod with the preparation of the Gospel of peace. In Christ Jesus I have peace, and pursue peace with all men. I am a minister of reconciliation proclaiming the good news of the Gospel.

I take the shield of faith, wherewith I am able to quench all the fiery darts of the wicked, the helmet of salvation *(holding the thoughts, feelings, and purpose of God's heart)* and the sword of the Spirit, which is the Word of God. In the face of all trials, tests, temptations and tribulation, I cut to pieces the snare of the enemy by speaking the Word of God. Greater is He that is in me than he that is in the world.

Thank You, Father, for the armor. I will pray at all times — on every occasion, in every season — in the Spirit, with all [manner of] prayer and entreaty. To that end I will keep alert and watch with strong purpose and perseverance, interceding in behalf of all the saints. My power and ability and sufficiency are from God Who has qualified me as a minister and a dispenser of a new covenant [of salvation through Christ]. Amen.

Scripture References

Ephesians 6:11-14a
John 17:17b
2 Corinthians 10:4
Ephesians 6:14b, 15 AMP
Ephesians 2:14

Psalm 34:14
2 Corinthians 5:18
Ephesians 6:16,17 AMP
1 John 4:4b
2 Corinthians 3:5,6 AMP

14
To Bear Fruit

Lord Jesus, You said in John 15:16 that You have chosen us and ordained us that we should go and bring forth fruit and that our fruit should remain, that whatsoever we shall ask of the Father in Your name, He may give it to us.

The Apostle Paul said to be filled with the fruit of righteousness and that he desired that fruit might abound to our account. Therefore, I commit myself to bring forth the fruit of the spirit: love, joy, peace, longsuffering, gentleness, goodness, faith, meekness, and temperance.

I renounce and turn from the fruit of the flesh, because I am Christ's and have crucified the flesh with its affections and lusts.

A seed cannot bear fruit unless it first falls into the ground and dies. I confess that I am crucified with Christ: nevertheless I live; yet not I but Christ lives in me. And the life that I now live in the flesh I live by the faith of the Son of God, Who loved me and gave Himself for me.

Father, I thank you that I am good ground, that I hear Your Word and understand it, and that the Word bears fruit in my life — sometimes a hundredfold, sometimes sixty, sometimes thirty. I am like a tree planted by the rivers of water that brings forth fruit in its season. My leaf shall not wither, and whatever I do shall prosper.

Father, thank You for filling me with the knowledge of Your will in all wisdom and spiritual understanding, that I may walk worthy of You, Lord, being fruitful in every good work and increasing in the knowledge of You.

Scripture References

John 15:16
Philippians 1:11
Philippians 4:17
Galatians 5:22-24
John 12:24

Galatians 2:20
Matthew 13:23
Psalm 1:3
Colossians 1:9,10

15
To Help Others

Father, in the name of Jesus, I will do unto others as I would have them do unto me. I eagerly pursue and seek to acquire [this] (*agape*) love — I make it my aim, my great quest in life.

Father, in the name of Jesus, I will esteem and look upon and be concerned for not [merely] my own interest, but also for the interest of others as they pursue success. I am strong in the Lord, and in the power of His might. I will, on purpose, in the name of Jesus, make it a practice to please (make happy) my neighbor, (*boss, co-worker, teacher, parent, child, brother, etc.*) for his good and for his true welfare, to edify him — that is, to strengthen him and build him up in all ways — spiritually, socially and materially.

Father, in the name of Jesus, I will therefore encourage (admonish, exhort) others and edify — strengthen and build up — others.

Father, in the name of Jesus, I love my enemies (*as well as my business associates, fellow church members, neighbors, those in authority over me*) and am kind and do good — doing favors so that someone derives benefit from them, I lend expecting and hoping for nothing in return, but considering nothing as lost and despairing of no one. Then my recompense (my reward) will be great — rich, strong, intense, and abundant — and I will be a son of the Most High; for He is kind and charitable and good to the ungrateful and selfish and wicked. I am merciful — sympathetic, tender, responsive, and compassionate —

To Help Others

even as my Father is [all these]. I am an imitator of God, my Father — therefore, I walk in love.

Thank You, Father, for imprinting Your laws upon my heart, and inscribing them on my mind — on my inmost thoughts and understanding. According to Your Word, as I would like and desire that men would do to me, I do exactly so to them, in the name of Jesus.

Scripture References

Luke 6:31
1 Corinthians 14:1 AMP
Philippians 2:4 AMP
Ephesians 6:10
Romans 15:2 AMP

1Thessalonians 5:11 AMP
Luke 6:35,36 AMP
Ephesians 5:1,2 AMP
Hebrews 10:16b AMP
Luke 6:31 AMP

16
To Walk in Love

Father, in Jesus' name, I thank You that the love of God has been poured forth into my heart by the Holy Spirit Who has been given to me. I keep and treasure Your Word. The love of and for You, Father, has been perfected and completed in me, and perfect love casts out all fear.

Father, I am Your child, and *I commit to walk in the God kind of love*. I endure long, am patient, and kind. I am never envious and never boil over with jealousy. I am not boastful or vainglorious, and I do not display myself haughtily. I am not rude and unmannerly and I do not act unbecomingly. I do not insist on my own rights or my own way for I am not self-seeking, touchy, fretful or resentful.

I take no account of an evil done to me and pay no attention to a suffered wrong. I do not rejoice at injustice and unrighteousness, but I rejoice when right and truth prevail. I bear up under anything and everything that comes. I am ever ready to believe the *best* of others. My hopes are fadeless under all circumstances. I endure everything without weakening because my love never fails.

Father, I *bless* and *pray* for those who persecute me — who are cruel in their attitude toward me. I bless them and do not curse them. Therefore, my love abounds yet more and more in knowledge and in all judgment. I approve things that are excellent. I am sincere and *without offense* till the day of Christ. I am filled with the fruits of righteousness.

Everywhere I go I commit to plant seeds of love. I thank You, Father, for preparing hearts ahead of time to receive this love. I know that these seeds will produce Your love in the hearts to whom they are given.

Father, I thank You that as I flow in Your love and wisdom, people are being blessed by my life and ministry. Father, You make me to find favor, compassion, and loving-kindness with others (*name them*).

I am rooted deep in love and founded securely on love knowing that You are on my side, and nothing is able to separate me from Your love, Father, which is in Christ Jesus my Lord. Thank you, Father, in Jesus' precious name. Amen.

Scripture References

Romans 5:5
1 John 2:5
1 John 4:18
1 Corinthians 13:4-8 AMP
Romans 12:14 AMP
Matthew 5:44

Philippians 1:9-11
John 13:34
1Corinthians 3:6
Daniel 1:9 AMP
Ephesians 3:17 AMP
Romans 8:31,39

17
To Walk in Forgiveness

Father, in the name of Jesus, I make a fresh commitment to You to live in peace and harmony, not only with the other brothers and sisters of the Body of Christ, but also with my friends, associates, neighbors, and family.

I let go of all bitterness, resentment, envying, strife, and unkindness in any form. I give no place to the devil in Jesus' name. Now Father, I ask for Your forgiveness. By faith, I receive it, having assurance that I am cleansed from all unrighteousness through Jesus Christ. I ask You to forgive and release all who have wronged and hurt me. I forgive and release them. Deal with them in your mercy and loving-kindness.

From this moment on, I purpose to walk in love, to seek peace, to live in agreement, and to conduct myself toward others in a manner that is pleasing to You. I know that I have right standing with you and Your ears are attentive to my prayers.

It is written in Your Word that the love of God has been poured forth into my heart by the Holy Ghost who is given to me. I believe that love flows forth into the lives of everyone I know, that I may be filled with and abound in the fruits of righteousness which bring glory and honor unto You, Lord, in Jesus' name. So be it!

To Walk in Forgiveness

Scripture References

Romans 12:16-18
Romans 12:10
Philippians 2:2
Ephesians 4:31
Ephesians 4:27
John 1:9

Mark 11:25
Ephesians 4:32
1 Peter 3:8,11,12
Colossians 1:10
Romans 5:5
Philippians 1:11 AMP

18
To Live Free From Worry

Father, I thank You that I have been delivered from the power of darkness and translated into the kingdom of Your dear Son. *I commit to live free from worry in the name of Jesus,* for the law of the Spirit of life in Christ Jesus has made me *free* from the law of sin and death.

I humble myself under Your mighty hand that in due time You may exalt me. I cast the whole of my cares (*name them*) — all my anxieties, all my worries, all my concerns, once and for all — on You. You care for me affectionately and care about me watchfully. You sustain me. You will never allow the consistently righteous to be moved — made to slip, fall, or fail!

Father, I delight myself in You, and You perfect that which concerns me.

I cast down imaginations (reasonings) and every high thing that exalts itself against the knowledge of You, and bring into captivity every thought to the obedience of Christ. I lay aside every weight and the sin of worry which does try so easily to beset me. I run with patience the race that is set before me, looking unto Jesus, the author and finisher of my faith.

I thank You, Father, that You are able to keep that which I have committed unto You. I think on (fix my mind on) those things that are true, honest, just, pure, lovely, of good report, virtuous, and deserving of praise. I let not my heart be troubled. I abide in Your Words, and Your Words abide in me. Therefore, Father, I do not forget what manner of person I am. I look into the perfect law of liberty and

To Live Free From Worry

continue therein, being *not* a forgetful hearer, but a *doer of the Word* and thus blessed in my doing!

Thank You, Father, *I am carefree*. I walk in that peace which passes all understanding in Jesus' name!

Scripture References

Colossians 1:13	Hebrews 12:1,2
Romans 8:2	2 Timothy 1:12
1 Peter 5:6,7 AMP	Philippians 4:8
Psalm 55:22	John 14:1
Psalm 37:4,5	John 15:7
Psalm 138:8	James 1:22-25
2 Corinthians 10:5	Philippians 4:6

19
To Receive Jesus as Savior and Lord

Father, it is written in Your Word that if I confess with my mouth that Jesus is Lord and believe in my heart that You have raised Him from the dead, I shall be saved. Therefore, Father, I confess that Jesus is my Lord. I make Him Lord of my life right now. I believe in my heart that You raised Jesus from the dead. I renounce my past life with Satan and close the door to any of his devices.

I thank You for forgiving me of all my sin. Jesus is my Lord, and I am a new creation. Old things have passed away. Now all things become new in Jesus' name. Amen.

Scripture References

John 3:16	John 14:6
John 6:37	Romans 10:9,10
John 10:10b	Romans 10:13
Romans 3:23	Ephesians 2:1-10
2 Corinthians 5:19	2 Corinthians 5:17
John 16:8,9	John 1:12
Romans 5:8	2 Corinthians 5:21

20
To Receive the Infilling of the Holy Spirit

My heavenly Father, I am Your child, for I believe in my heart that Jesus has been raised from the dead, and I have confessed Him as my Lord.

Jesus said, "How much more shall your heavenly Father give the Holy Spirit to those who ask Him." I ask You now in the name of Jesus to fill me with the Holy Spirit. I step into the fullness and power that I desire in the name of Jesus. I confess that I am a Spirit-filled Christian. As I yield my vocal organs, I expect to speak in tongues for the Spirit gives me utterance in the name of Jesus. Praise the Lord!

Scripture References

John 14:16,17	Acts 10:44-46
Luke 11:13	Acts 19:2,5,6
Acts 1:8a	1 Corinthians 14:2-15
Acts 2:4	1 Corinthians 14:18,27
Acts 2:32,33,39	Ephesians 6:18
Acts 8:12-17	Jude 1:20

21
Prosperity

Father, in the name of Your Son, Jesus, I confess Your Word over my finances this day. As I do this, I say it with my mouth and believe it in my heart and know that Your Word will not return to You void, but will accomplish what it says it will do.

Therefore, I believe in the name of Jesus that all my needs are met, according to Philippians 4:19. I believe that because I have given tithes and offerings to further your cause, Father, gifts will be given to me, good measure, pressed down, shaken together, and running over will they pour into my bosom. For with the measure I deal out, it will be measured back to me.

Father, You have delivered me out of the authority of darkness into the Kingdom of Your dear Son. Father, I have taken my place as your child. I thank You that You have assumed Your place as my Father and have made Your home with me. You are taking care of me and even now are enabling me to walk in love and in wisdom, and to walk in the fullness of fellowship with Your Son.

Satan, I bind you from my finances, according to Matthew 18:18, and loose you from your assignment against me, in the name of Jesus.

Father, I thank You that Your ministering spirits are now free to minister for me and bring in the necessary finances.

Father, I confess You are a very present help in trouble, and You are more than enough. I confess, God, You are able

Prosperity

to make all grace — every favor and earthly blessing — come to me in abundance, so that I am always, and in all circumstances furnished in abundance for every good work and charitable donation.

Scripture References

Isaiah 55:11	2 Corinthians 6:16,18
Philippians 4:19	Matthew 18:18
Luke 6:38	Hebrews 1:14
Mark 10:29,30	2 Corinthians 9:8 AMP
Colossians 1:13	Psalm 46:1

22
Dedication of Your Tithes

I profess this day unto the Lord God that I have come into the inheritance which the Lord swore to give me. I am in the land which You have provided for me in Jesus Christ, the Kingdom of Almighty God. I was a sinner serving Satan; he was my god. But I called upon the name of Jesus, and You heard my cry and delivered me into the Kingdom of Your dear Son.

Jesus, as my Lord and High Priest, I bring the first fruits of my income to You and worship the Lord my God with it.

I rejoice in all the good which You have given to me and my household. I have hearkened to the voice of the Lord my God and have done according to all that He has commanded me. Now look down from your holy habitation from heaven and bless me as You said in Your Word. I thank You, Father, in Jesus' name.

Scripture Reference
Deuteronomy 26:1,3,10,11,14,15 AMP   Colossians 1:13
Ephesians 2:1-5

23
Being Equipped for Success

Father, I thank You that the entrance of Your words gives light. I thank You that Your Word which You speak (*and which I speak*) is alive and full of power — making it active, operative, energizing, and effective. I thank You, Father, that [You have given me a spirit] of power, and of love, and of a calm and well-balanced mind, and discipline, and self-control. I have Your power and ability and sufficiency, for You have qualified me (making me to be fit and worthy and sufficient) as a minister and dispenser of a new covenant [of salvation through Christ].

In the name of Jesus, I walk out of the realm of failure into the arena of success, giving thanks to You, Father, for You have qualified and made me fit to share the portion which is the inheritance of the saints (God's holy people) in the Light.

Father, You have delivered and drawn me to Yourself out of the control and the dominion of darkness (*failure, doubt and fear*) and have transferred me into the Kingdom of the Son of Your love, in Whom there is good success [and freedom from fears, agitating passions, and moral conflicts]. I rejoice in Jesus Who has come that I might have life and have it more abundantly.

Today I am a new creation, for I am (ingrafted) in Christ, the Messiah. The old (previous moral and spiritual condition) has passed away. Behold, the fresh and new has come! I forget those things which are behind me and reach forth unto those things which are before me. I am crucified with Christ: nevertheless I live; yet not I, but Christ lives in me: and the life which I now live in the flesh I live by the faith of the Son of God, Who loved me, and gave Himself for me.

Today I attend to the Word of God. I consent and submit to Your sayings, Father. Your words shall not depart from my sight; I will keep them in the midst of my heart. For they are life (*success*) to me, healing and health to all my flesh. I keep my heart with all vigilance and above all that I guard, for out of it flow the springs of life.

Today I will not let mercy and kindness and truth forsake me. I bind them about my neck; I write them upon the tablet of my heart. So therefore I will find favor, good understanding, and high esteem in the sight [or judgment] of God and man.

Today my delight and desire are in the law of the Lord, and on His law I habitually meditate (ponder and study) by day and by night. Therefore I am like a tree firmly placed [and tended] by the streams of water, ready to bring forth my fruit in my season; my leaf also shall not fade or wither, and everything I do shall prosper [and come to maturity].

Now thanks be to God, Who always causes me to triumph in Christ!

Scripture References

Psalm 119:130
Hebrews 4:12a AMP
2 Timothy 1:7b AMP
2 Corinthians 3:5b-6a AMP
Colossians 1:12,13 AMP
2 Corinthians 5:17 AMP

John 10:10b
Philippians 3:13b
Galatians 2:20
Proverbs 4:20-23 AMP
Proverbs 3:3,4 AMP
Psalm 1:2,3 AMP
2 Corinthians 2:14

24
The Body of Christ

Father, we pray and confess Your Word over the Body of Christ. We pray that Your people be filled with the full, deep, and clear knowledge of Your will in all spiritual things. We pray they live and conduct themselves in a manner worthy of You, Lord, fully pleasing to You and desiring to please You in all things, bearing fruit in every good work, and steadily growing and increasing in and by the knowledge of You, with fuller, deeper, and clearer insight.

We pray that the Body of Christ will be invigorated and strengthened with all power, according to the might of Your glory, to exercise every kind of endurance and patience with joy, giving thanks to You, Father, Who has qualified and made them fit to share the portion which is the inheritance of the saints (God's holy people) in the Light. You, Father, have delivered and drawn them to Yourself out of the control and the dominion of darkness and have transferred them into the Kingdom of the Son of Your love, in Whom they have their redemption through His blood, which means the remission of their sins.

Father, You delight at the sight of the Body of Christ, standing shoulder to shoulder in such orderly array and the firmness and the solid front and steadfastness of their faith in Christ, leaning on Him in absolute trust and confidence in His power, wisdom, and goodness. They walk — regulate their lives and conduct themselves — in union with and conformity to Him, having the roots of their being firmly and deeply planted in Him, being continually built up in

Him, becoming increasingly more confirmed and established in the faith.

Your people, Father, clothe themselves as Your own picked representatives — Your chosen ones, who are purified and holy and well-beloved by You — by putting on behavior marked by tender-hearted pity and mercy, kind feeling, gentle ways, and patience. They have the power to endure whatever comes, with good temper. They are gentle and forbearing with each other and, if they have a grievance or complaint against another, readily pardon each other. As You, Lord, have freely forgiven them, so do they also forgive.

Your people put on love and enfold themselves with the bond of perfectness — which binds everything together completely in ideal harmony. They let the peace from Jesus act as umpire continually in their hearts — deciding and settling with all finality all the questions that arise in their minds — in that peaceful state to which they are called. They are thankful, appreciative, giving praise to You always.

The Body of Christ lets the Word spoken by Christ the Messiah have its home in their hearts and minds. It dwells in them in all richness, as they teach, admonish, and train each other in all insight, intelligence, and wisdom in spiritual songs, making melody to You, Father, with Your grace in their hearts.

And whatever they do in word or deed, they do everything in the name of the Lord Jesus and in dependence upon His person, giving praise to You, Father, through Him!

Scripture References (AMP)

Colossians 1:9-14   Colossians 2:5-7
Colossians 3:12-17

25
Ministers

Father, in the name of Jesus, we pray and confess that the Spirit of the Lord shall rest upon_____... the spirit of wisdom and understanding, the spirit of counsel and might, the spirit of knowledge. We pray that as Your Spirit rests upon _____ He will make him/her quick understanding because You, Lord, have anointed and qualified him/her to preach the Gospel to the meek, the poor, the afflicted. You have sent _____ to bind up and heal the brokenhearted, to proclaim liberty to the physical and spiritual captives, and the opening of the prison and of the eyes to those who are bound.

_____ shall be called the priest of the Lord. People will speak of him/her as a minister of God. He/she shall eat the wealth of the nation.

We pray and believe that no weapon that is formed against _____ shall prosper and that any tongue that rises against him/her in judgment shall be shown to be in the wrong. We pray that You prosper _____ abundantly, Lord — physically, spiritually, and financially.

We confess that _____ holds fast and follows the pattern of wholesome and sound teaching in all faith and love which is for us in Christ Jesus.

_____ guards and keeps with the greatest love the precious and excellently adapted Truth which has been entrusted to him/her by the Holy Spirit Who makes His home in _____.

Lord, we pray and believe that, each and every day, freedom of utterance is given _____, that he/she

Prayers for God's People

will open his/her mouth boldly and courageously as he/she ought to do to get the Gospel to the people.

Thank You, Lord, for the added strength which comes superhumanly that You have given him/her.

We hereby confess that we shall stand behind _____ and undergird him/her in prayer. We will say only that good thing that will edify_____.

We will not allow ourselves to judge him/her, but will continue to intercede for him/her and speak and pray blessings upon him/her in the name of Jesus.

Thank You, Jesus, for the answers. Hallelujah!

Scripture References

Isaiah 11:2,3	2 Timothy 1:13,14 AMP
Isaiah 61:1,6 AMP	Ephesians 6:19,20 AMP
Isaiah 54:17 AMP	1 Peter 3:12

26
Church Teachers

Father, we come in the name of Jesus, asking You for called teachers for our classes and choirs. We thank You for teachers who are filled with the Spirit of God, in wisdom and ability, in understanding and intelligence, in knowledge, and in all kinds of craftsmanship, to devise skillful methods for teaching us and our children the Word of God. They are teachers who give themselves to teaching.

Father, may these teachers recognize that they must assume the greater accountability. According to Your Word, teachers will be judged by a higher standard and with greater severity [than other people]. We thank You that our teachers will not offend in speech — never say the wrong things — that they may be fully developed characters and perfect men and women, each one able to control his/her own body and to curb his/her entire nature.

Thank You that our teachers are part of the fivefold ministry who are perfecting and fully equipping the saints (God's consecrated people), [that they should do] the work of ministering toward building up Christ's Body (the church), [that it might develop] until we all attain oneness in the faith and in the comprehension of the full and accurate knowledge of the Son of God; that [we might arrive] at really mature manhood — the completeness of personality which is nothing less than the standard height of Christ's own perfection — the measure of the stature of the fullness of the Christ, and the completeness found in Him.

Thank You, Father, that Your people at our church are no longer children, tossed [like ships] to and fro. They are enfolded in love, growing up in every way and in all things to Him, Who is the head, [even] Christ, the Messiah, the Anointed One.

Father, You are effectually at work in our teachers — energizing and creating in them the power and desire — both to will and to work for Your good pleasure and satisfaction and delight. Father, in the name of Jesus, their power and ability and sufficiency are from You. [It is You] Who have qualified them (making them to be fit, worthy and sufficient) as ministers and dispensers of a new covenant. They are not ministers of the law which kills, but of the (Holy) Spirit which makes alive.

Father, we rejoice in the Lord over our teachers and commit to undergird them with our faith and love. We will not judge or criticize them, but speak excellent and princely things concerning them. The opening of our lips shall be for right things.

Thank You, Father, that the teachers live in harmony, with the other members of our church, being in full accord and of one harmonious mind and intention. Each is not [merely] concerned for his/her own interests, but each for the interest of others. Jesus is our example in humility, and our teachers shall tend — nurture, guard, guide, and fold — the flock of God which is [their responsibility], and will be examples of Christian living to the flock (the congregation).

Thank You, Father, for the performance of Your Word in our midst, in the name of Jesus.

Scripture References (AMP)

Exodus 31:3,4
Romans 12:7
James 3:1,2
Ephesians 4:12-15
Philippians 2:13
2 Corinthians 3:5b,6
Proverbs 8:6
Philippians 2:2,4,5
1 Peter 5:2,3
Jeremiah 1:12

27
Missionaries

Father, we lift before You those in the Body of Christ who are out in the field carrying the good news of the Gospel — not only in this country but also around the world. We lift those in the Body of Christ who are suffering persecution — those who are in prison for their beliefs. Father, we know that You watch over Your Word to perform it, that Your Word prospers in the thing for which You sent it. Therefore, we speak Your Word and establish Your covenant on this earth. We pray here and others receive the answer there by the Holy Spirit.

Thank You, Father, for revealing unto Your people the integrity of Your Word and that they must be firm in faith against the devil's onset, withstanding him. Father, You are their light, salvation, refuge, and stronghold. You hide them in Your shelter and set them high upon a rock. It is Your will that each one prospers, is in good health, and lives in victory. You set the prisoners free, feed the hungry, execute justice, rescue, and deliver.

In Jesus' name, we bind you, Satan, and every menacing spirit that would stir up against God's people.

We commission the ministering spirits to go forth and provide the necessary help for and assistance to these heirs of salvation. We and they are strong in the Lord and in the power of Your might, quenching every dart of the devil in Jesus' name.

Father, we use our faith covering these in the Body of Christ with Your Word. We say that no weapon formed against them shall prosper, and any tongue that rises against them in judgment they shall show to be in the wrong. This peace, security, and triumph over opposition is their inheritance as Your children. This is the righteousness which they obtain from You, Father, which You impart to them as their justification. They are far from even the thought of destruction, for they shall not fear and terror shall not come near them.

Father, You say You will establish them to the end — keep them steadfast, give them strength, and guarantee their vindication, that is, be their warrant against all accusation or indictment. They are not anxious beforehand how they shall reply in defense or what they are to say, for the Holy Spirit teaches them in that very hour and moment what they ought to say to those in the outside world, their speech being seasoned with salt.

We commit these our brothers and sisters in the Lord to You, Father, deposited into Your charge, entrusting them to Your protection and care, for You are faithful. You strengthen them and set them on a firm foundation and guard them from the evil one. We join our voices in praise unto You, Most High, that You might silence the enemy and avenger. Praise the Lord! Greater is He Who is in us than he who is in the world!

Scripture References

Jeremiah 1:12
Isaiah 55:11
1 Peter 5:9 AMP
Psalm 27:1,5 AMP
3 John 2
Psalm 146:7
Matthew 18:18
Hebrews 1:14
1 John 4:4

Ephesians 6:10,16
Isaiah 54:14,17 AMP
1 Corinthians 1:8 AMP
Luke 12:11,12 AMP
Colossians 4:6
Acts 20:32
2 Thessalonians 3:3 AMP
Psalm 8:2 AMP

28
Success of a Meeting

Father, in the name of Jesus, we openly confess that the Word of God will come forth boldly and accurately during the _____ (meeting) and that the people who hear Your word will not be able to resist the wisdom and the inspiration of the Holy Spirit that will be spoken through Your minister(s) of the Gospel.

We confess that, as Your Word comes forth, an anointing of the Holy Spirit will cause people to open their spiritual eyes and ears and turn from darkness to light — from the power of Satan to You, God, and make Jesus their Lord.

We commit this meeting to You, Father, we deposit it into Your charge — entrusting this meeting, the people who will hear, and the people will speak into Your protection and care. We commend this meeting to the Word — the commands and counsels and promises of Your unmerited favor. Father, we know Your Word will build up the people and cause them to realize that they are joint-heirs with Jesus.

We believe, Father, that as Your Word comes forth, an anointing will be upon the speaker and _____ (name) will be submitted completely to the Holy Spirit, for the Word of God that is spoken is alive and full of power, making it active, operative, energizing, and effective, being sharper than any two-edged sword. We believe that every need of every person will be met spiritually, physically, mentally, and financially.

We thank You, Father, and praise You that, because we have asked and agreed together, these petitions have come to pass. Let these words with which we have made supplication before the Lord be near to the Lord our God day and night, that He may maintain the cause and right of His people in the _____ (<u>meeting</u>) as each day of it requires! We believe that all the earth's people will know that the Lord is God and there is no other! Hallelujah!

Scripture References (AMP)

Acts 6:10	Hebrews 4:12
Acts 26:18	Matthew 18:19
Acts 20:32	1 Kings 8:59,60

29
Vision For a Church

Father, in the name of Jesus, we come into Your presence thanking You for _____ (name of church). You have called us to be saints in_____ (name of city) and around the world. As we lift our voices in one accord, we recognize that You are God, and everything was made by and for You. We call into being those things that be not as though they were.

We thank You that we all speak the same thing: there is no division among us; we are perfectly joined together in the same mind. Grant unto us, Your representatives here, a boldness to speak Your Word which You will confirm with signs following. We thank You that we have workmen in abundance and all manner of cunning people for every manner of work. Each department operates in the excellence of ministry and intercessions. We have in our church the ministry gifts of the edifying of this body till we all come into the unity of the faith, and the knowledge of the Son of God, unto a mature person. None of our people will be children, tossed to and fro, carried about with every wind of doctrine. We speak the truth in love.

We are a growing and witnessing body of believers becoming _____ (number) strong. We have every need met. Therefore, we meet the needs of people who come — spirit, soul, and body. We ask for the wisdom of God in meeting these needs. Father, we thank You for the ministry facilities that will more than meet the needs of the ministry You have called us to. Our church is prospering financially, and we have more than enough to meet every situation. We have everything we need to carry out Your Great Commission and reach the _____ (name of city or county) area for Jesus. We are a people of love as love is shed abroad in our hearts by the Holy Spirit. We thank You that the Word of God is living big in all of us and Jesus is Lord!

We are a supernatural church, composed of supernatural people doing supernatural things, for we are laborers together with God. We thank You for Your presence among us and we lift our hands and praise Your Holy name!

Scripture References

Acts 4:24	Ephesians 4:11-15
Romans 4:17	Philippians 4:19
1 Corinthians 1:10	Romans 5:5
Acts 4:29	1 Corinthians 3:9
Mark 16:20b	Psalm 63:4
Exodus 35:33	

This prayer was written by and used with the permission of T. R. King; Valley Christian Center; Roanoke, Virginia.

30
Revival

Father, in the name of Jesus, You have revived us again that Your people may rejoice in You. Thank You for showing us Your mercy and lovingkindness, O Lord, and for granting us Your salvation. You have created in us a clean heart, O God, and renewed a right, persevering and steadfast spirit within us. You have restored unto us the joy of Your salvation, and You are upholding us with a willing spirit. Now we will teach transgressors Your ways, and sinners shall be converted and return to You.

We therefore cleanse our ways by taking heed and keeping watch [on ourselves] according to Your Word [conforming our lives to it]. Since Your [great] promises are ours, we cleanse ourselves from everything that contaminates and defiles our bodies and spirits, and bring [our] consecration to completeness in the (reverential) fear of God. With our whole hearts have we sought You, inquiring for You and of You, and yearning for You; O let us not wander or step aside [either in ignorance or willfully] from Your commandments. Your Word have we laid up in our hearts, that we might not sin against You.

Jesus, thank You for cleansing us through the Word — the teachings — which You have given us.

We delight ourselves in Your statutes; we will not forget Your Word. Deal bountifully with Your servants, that we may live; and we will observe Your Word [hearing, receiving, loving, and obeying it].

Father, in the name of Jesus, we are doers of the Word, and not merely listeners to it. It is You, O Most High, Who has revived and stimulated us according to Your Word! Thank You for turning away our eyes from beholding vanity [idols and idolatry]; and restoring us to vigorous life and health in Your ways. Behold, we long for Your precepts; in Your righteousness give us renewed life. This is our comfort and consolation in our affliction, that Your Word has revived us and given us life.

We strip ourselves of our former natures — put off and discard our old unrenewed selves — which characterized our previous manner of life. We are constantly renewed in the spirit of our minds — having a fresh mental and spiritual attitude; and we put on the new nature (the regenerate self) created in God's image, (Godlike) in true righteousness and holiness. Though our outer man is (progressively) decaying and wasting away, our inner self is being (progressively) renewed day after day. Hallelujah!

Scripture References (AMP)

Psalm 85:6,7	James 1:22
Psalm 51:10,12,13	Psalm 119:25
Psalm 119:9-11	Psalm 119:37,40,50
2 Corinthians 7:1	Ephesians 4:22-24
John 15:3	2 Corinthians 4:16b
Psalm 119:16,17	

31
Unity and Harmony

Father, in the name of Jesus, this is the confidence that we have in You, that, if we ask anything according to Your will, You hear us: and since we know that You hear us, whatsoever we ask, we know that we have the petitions that we desire of You.

Father, You said, **Behold, they are of one people, and they have all one language; and this is only the beginning of what they will do; and now nothing they have imagined they can do will be impossible to them** (Gen. 11:6 AMP). We pray by the name of our Lord Jesus, that all of us in Your Body be in perfect harmony, and full agreement in what we say, and that there be no dissensions or factions or divisions among us; but that we be perfectly united in our common understanding and in our opinions and judgments.

Holy Spirit, teach us how to agree (harmonize together, together make a symphony) about — anything and everything — so that whatever we ask will come to pass and be done for us by our Father in heaven.

We pray that as members of the Body of Christ we will live as becomes us — with complete lowliness of mind (humility) and meekness (unselfishness, gentleness, mildness), with patience, bearing with one another and making allowances because we love one another. In the name of Jesus, we are eager and strive earnestly to guard and keep the harmony and oneness of [produced by] the Spirit in the binding power of peace.

We commit, in the name of Jesus, and according to the power of God at work in us, to be of one and the same mind (united in spirit), sympathizing [with one another], loving [each the others] as brethren (of one household), compassionate and courteous — tenderhearted and humble-minded. We will never return evil for evil or insult for insult — scolding, tongue-lashing, berating; but on the contrary blessing — praying for their welfare, happiness, and protection, and truly pitying and loving one another. For we know that to this we have been called, that we may ourselves inherit a blessing [from God] — obtain a blessing as heirs, bringing welfare and happiness and protection.

Father, thank You that Jesus has given to us the glory and honor which You gave Him, that we may be one, [even] as You and Jesus are one: Jesus in us and You in Jesus, in order that we may become one and perfectly united, that the world may know and [definitely] recognize that You sent Jesus, and that You have loved them [even] as You have loved Jesus.

Father, Thy will be done in earth, as it is in heaven. Amen, and so be it.

Scripture References

1 John 5:14,15
Genesis 11:6 AMP
1 Corinthians 1:10 AMP
Matthew 18:19 AMP

Ephesians 4:2,3 AMP
1 Peter 3:8,9 AMP
John 17:22,23 AMP
Matthew 6:10b

32
Personal Prayer of a Pastor for the Congregation

Father, as the pastor of _____, I approach the throne of grace on behalf of the membership. I thank my God in all my remembrance of them. In every prayer of mine I always make my entreaty and petition for them all with joy (delight). [I thank God] for their fellowship — their sympathetic co-operation and contributions and partnership — in advancing the good news (the Gospel). And I am convinced and sure of this very thing, that You have begun a good work in them and will continue until the day of Jesus Christ — developing [that good work] and perfecting and bringing it to full completion in them.

In the name of Jesus, it is right and appropriate for me to have this confidence and feel this way about them all, because even as they do me, I hold them in my heart as partakers and sharers, one and all with me, of grace (God's unmerited favor and spiritual blessing).

Father, You are my witness and know how I long for and pursue them all with love, in the tender mercies of Christ Jesus [Himself]!

And this I pray, that their love may abound yet more and more and extend to its fullest development in knowledge and all keen insight — that is, that their love may [display itself in] greater depth of acquaintance and more comprehensive discernment; so that they may surely learn to sense what is vital, and approve and prize what is excellent and of real value — recognizing the highest and

Prayers for God's People

best, and distinguishing the moral difference. I pray that they may be untainted and pure and unerring and blameless, that — with hearts sincere and certain and unsullied — they may [approach] the day of Christ, not stumbling nor causing others to stumble.

Father, may the membership abound in and be filled with the fruits of righteousness (of right standing with God and right doing) which comes through Jesus Christ, the Anointed One, to the honor and praise of God — that Your glory may be both manifested and recognized.

I commit myself to You, Father, anew and to them, for I am convinced of this, I shall remain and stay by them all, to promote their progress and joy in believing, so that in me they may have abundant cause for exultation and glorifying in Christ Jesus. In the name of Jesus, they will be sure as citizens so to conduct themselves that their manner of life will be worthy of the good news (the Gospel) of Christ.

Thank You, Father, that they are standing firm in united spirit and purpose, striving side by side and contending with a single mind for the faith of the glad tidings (the Gospel). They are not for a moment frightened or intimidated in anything by their opponents and adversaries, for such [constancy and fearlessness] will be a clear sign (proof and seal) to their enemies of [their impending] destruction; but [a sure token and evidence] to the congregation of their deliverance and salvation, and that from You, God.

The membership of _____ fills up and completes my joy by living in harmony and being of the same mind and one in purpose, having the same love, being in full accord and of one harmonious mind and intention.

Scripture References (AMP)
Philippians 1:4-7a,8-11,25,26,27,28   Philippians 2:2

33
Salvation of the Lost

Father, it is written in Your Word, **First of all, then I admonish and urge that petitions, prayers, intercessions and thanksgivings be offered on behalf of all men** (1 Timothy 2:1 AMP).

Therefore, Father, we bring the lost of the world this day — every man, woman, and child from here to the farthest corner of the earth — before You. As we intercede, we use our faith believing that thousands this day have the opportunity to make Jesus their Lord.

For everyone who has that opportunity, Satan, we bind your blinding spirit of antichrist and loose you from your assignment against those who have that opportunity to make Jesus Lord.

We ask the Lord of the harvest to thrust the perfect laborers across these lives this day to share the good news of the Gospel in a special way so that they will listen and understand it. We believe that they will not be able to resist the wooing of the Holy Spirit, for You, Father, bring them to repentance by Your goodness and love.

We confess that they shall see who have never been told of Jesus. They shall understand who have never heard of Jesus. And they shall come out of the snare of the devil who has held them captive. They shall open their eyes and turn from darkness to light — from the power of Satan to You, God!

Scripture References

1 Timothy 2:1 AMP
Matthew 18:18
Matthew 9:38

Romans 2:4
Romans 15:21 AMP
2 Timothy 2:26 AMP

34
Nations and Continents

Father, in the name of Jesus, we bring before You the nation (or continent) of _____ and its leaders. Father, You say in Your Word that You reprove leaders for our sakes so that we may live a quiet and peaceable life in all godliness and honesty.

We pray that skillful and godly wisdom has entered into the heart of _____ leaders and that knowledge is pleasant to them, that discretion watches over them and understanding keeps them and delivers them from the way of evil and from the evil men.

We pray that the upright shall dwell in the government(s) . . . that men and women of integrity, blameless and complete in Your sight, Father, shall remain, but the wicked shall be cut off and the treacherous shall be rooted out. We pray that those in authority winnow the wicked from among the good and bring the threshing wheel over them to separate the chaff from the grain, for loving-kindness and mercy, truth and faithfulness preserve those in authority and their offices are upheld by the people's loyalty.

We confess and believe that the decisions made by the leaders are divinely directed by You, Father, and their mouths should not transgress in judgment. Therefore, the leaders are men and women of discernment, understanding, and knowledge so the stability of _____ will long continue. We pray that the uncompromisingly righteous be in authority in _____ so that the people there can rejoice.

Prayers for the World

Father, it is an abomination for leaders to commit wickedness. We pray that their offices be established and made secure by righteousness and that right and just lips are a delight to those in authority and that they love those who speak what is right.

We pray and believe that the good news of the Gospel is published in this land. We thank You for laborers of the harvest to publish Your Word that Jesus is Lord in _____. We thank You for raising up intercessors to pray for _____ in Jesus' name. Amen.

Scripture References

1 Timothy 2:1,2	Proverbs 16:10,12,13 AMP
Proverbs 2:10-15 AMP	Proverbs 28:2
Proverbs 2:21,22 AMP	Proverbs 29:2
Proverbs 20:26,28 AMP	Psalm 68:11

Here is a list of continents and nations to help you as you pray for the world:

Continents:
- Africa
- Asia
- Europe
- North America
- Oceania
- South America

Nations and Commonwealths
- Afghanistan
- Albania
- Algeria
- Andorra
- Angola
- Antigua and Barbuda
- Argentina
- Armenia
- Australia
- Austria
- Ayerbaijan
- Bahamas
- Bahrain
- Bangladesh
- Barbados
- Belarus
- Belgium
- Belize
- Benin
- Bermuda
- Bhutan
- Bosnia-Herzegovinia

Bolivia
Botswana
Brazil
Brunei
Bulgaria
Burkina Faso
Burma
Burundi
Cambodia
Cameroon
Canada
Cape Verde
Central African Republic
Chad
Chile
China, People's
  Republic of
Colombia
Commonwealth of
  Independent States
  (Formerly USSR)
Comoros
Congo
Corsica
Costa Rica
Croatia
Cuba
Cyprus
Czecho
Denmark
Djibouti
Dominica
Dominican Republic
Ecuador
Egypt
El Salvador
Equatorial Guinea

Eritrea
Estonia
Ethiopia
Falkland Islands
Fiji
Finland
France
French Guiana
French Polynesia
Gabon
Gambia
Georgia
Federal Republic of
  Germany
Ghana
Gibraltar
Great Britain
Greece
Greenland
Grenada
Guadeloupe
Guatemala
Guinea
Guinea-Bissau
Guyana
Haiti
Honduras
Hong King
Hungary
Iceland
India
Indonesia
Iran
Iraq
Ireland
Israel
Italy

Prayers for the World

Ivory Coast
Jamaica
Japan
Jordan
Kazakhstan
Kenya
Kiribati
Korea, Democratic
  People's Republic
  (North)
Korea, Republic of (South)
Kuwait
Kyrgyzstan
Laos
Latvia
Lebanon
Lesotho
Liberia
Libya
Liechtenstein
Lithuania
Luxembourg
Macedonia
Madagascar
Madeira Islands
Malawi
Malaysia
Maldives
Mali
Malta
Martinique-Marshall
  Islands
Mauritania
Mauritius
Mexico
Micronesia
Moldovia
Monaco

Mongolia
Morocco
Mozambique
Myanmar
Nemibia
Nauru
Nepal
Netherlands
Netherlands Antiles
New Caledonia
New Zealand
Nicaragua
Niger
Nigeria
Norway
Oman
Pakistan
Panama
Papua New Guinea
Paraguay
Peru
Philippines
Pitcairn Island
Poland
Portugal
Qatar
Reunion
Romania
Russia
Rwanda
St. Christopher and
  Navis
St. Lucia
St. Vincent &
  The Grenadines
San Marino, Sao Tome
  and Principe
Saudi Arabia

Nations and Continents

Senegal	Trinidad & Tobago
Seychelles	Tunisia
Sierre Leona	Turkey
Singapore	Turkmenistan
Solomon Islands	Tuvalu (Ellice Islands)
Somalia	Uganda
South Africa	Ukraine
Spain	United Arab Emirates
Sri Lanka	United States of America
Sudan	Uruguay
Suriname	Uzbekistan
Swaziland	Vanualu
Sweden	Vatican City State
Switzerland	Venezuela
Syria	Vietnam
Taiwan	Western Samoa
Tajikistan	Yemen
Tanzania	Yugoslavia
Thailand	Zaire
Togo	Zambia
Tonga	Zimbabwe

35
Protection From Terrorism

Father, in the name of Jesus, we praise You and offer up thanksgiving because the Lord is near — He is coming soon. Therefore, we will not fret or have any anxiety about the terrorism that is threatening the lives of those who travel and those stationed on foreign soil or at home. But in this circumstance and in everything by prayer and petition [definite requests] with thanksgiving we continue to make our wants known to You.

Father, our petition is that terrorism in the heavenlies and on earth be stopped before it spreads to other countries and comes to our land, _____.

Jesus, You have given us the authority and power to trample upon serpents and scorpions, and (physical and mental strength and ability) over all the power that the enemy [possesses], and nothing shall in any way harm us.

Therefore, in the name of Jesus, we address and take authority over the prince of the power of the air and over the principalities, powers, the rulers of the darkness of this world, and spiritual wickedness in high places who have been assigned by Satan to terrorize God-fearing governments and their people.

Satan, we bind your works and render them null and void in the name of Jesus Christ of Nazareth, and we forbid you to operate in_____. We cast you out of our land and other God-fearing countries and command you to turn back in this day as we cry out; for this we know, that God is for us — and if God be for us who can be against us?

In the name of Jesus, we take authority over a spirit of timidity — of cowardice, of craven and cringing and fawning fear (of terrorism) — for [God has given us a spirit] of power and of love and of calm and well-balanced mind and discipline and self-control.

We shall not be afraid of the terror of the night, nor of the arrow [the evil plots and slanders of the wicked] that flies by day, nor of the pestilence that stalks in darkness, nor of the destruction and sudden death that surprise and lay waste at noonday.

Therefore, we establish ourselves on righteousness — right, in conformity with God's will and order; we shall be far even from the thought of oppression or destruction, for we shall not fear; and from terror, for it shall not come near us.

Holy Spirit, thank You for writing this Word upon the tables of our hearts so that we can speak it out of our mouths, for we will order our conversation aright and You will show us the salvation of God. Hallelujah!

Scripture References

Philippians 4:5,6b AMP
Luke 10:19 AMP
Ephesians 6:12 AMP
Matthew 16:19
Psalm 56:9 AMP
Romans 8:31b

2 Timothy 1:7 AMP
Psalm 91:5,6
Isaiah 54:14 AMP
Proverbs 3:3b AMP
Paslm 50:23

36
Protection and Deliverance of a City

Father, in the name of Jesus, we have received Your power — ability, efficiency, and might — because the Holy Spirit has come upon us; and we are Your witnesses in _____ and to the ends — the very bounds — of the earth.

We fearlessly and confidently and boldly draw near to the throne of grace that we may receive mercy and find grace to help in good time for every need — appropriate help and well-timed help, coming just when we in the city of _____ need it.

Father, thank You for sending forth Your commandments to the earth; Your Word runs very swiftly throughout _____. Your Word continues to grow and spread.

Father, we seek — inquire for, require and request — the peace and welfare of _____ in which You have caused us to live. We pray to You for the welfare of this city and do our part by getting involved in it. We will not let [false] prophets and diviners who are in our midst deceive us; we pay no attention and attach no significance to our dreams which we dream, or to theirs. Destroy [their schemes], O Lord; confuse their tongues; for we have seen violence and strife in the city.

Holy Spirit, we ask You to visit our city and open the eyes of the people, that they may turn from darkness to light, and from the power of Satan to God, so that they may

Protection and Deliverance of a City

thus receive forgiveness and release from their sins and a place and portion among those who are consecrated and purified by faith in Jesus.

Father, we pray for deliverance and salvation for those who are following the course and fashion of this world — who are under the sway of the tendency of this present age — following the prince of the power of the air.

Father, forgive them, for they know not what they do.

We speak to the prince of the power of the air, to the god of this world who blinds the unbelievers' minds (that they should not discern the truth), and we command that he leave the heavens above our city.

Thank You, Father, for the guardian angels assigned to this place who war for us in the heavenlies.

In the name of Jesus, we stand victorious over the principalities, powers, rulers of the darkness of this world, and spiritual wickedness in high places over _____.

Father, You said that morning after morning You will root up all the wicked in the land, that You may eliminate all the evildoers from the city of the Lord. We ask the Holy Spirit to sweep through the gates of our city and convince the people and bring demonstration to them about sin and about righteousness — uprightness of heart and right standing with God — and about judgment.

Father, You said, **For I know the thoughts and plans that I have for you, . . . thoughts and plans for welfare and peace, and not for evil, to give you hope in your final outcome** (Jer. 29:11 AMP). By the blessing of the influence of the upright and God's favor [because of them] the city of _____ is exalted.

Prayers for the World

Scripture References

Acts 1:8 AMP
Hebrews 4:16 AMP
Psalm 147:15 AMP
Acts 12:24 AMP
Jeremiah 29:7,8 AMP
Psalm 55:9 AMP
Acts 26:18 AMP
Ephesians 2:2 AMP

Luke 23:34a AMP
2 Corinthians 4:4 AMP
Ephesians 6:12
Psalm 101:8 AMP
John 16:8 AMP
Jeremiah 29:11 AMP
Proverbs 11:11a AMP

37
American Government

Father, in Jesus' name, we give thanks for the United States and its government. We hold up in prayer before You the men and women who are in positions of authority. We pray and intercede for the president, the vice president, the representatives, the senators, the judges of our land, the policemen, as well as the governors and mayors, and for all those who are in authority over us in any way. We pray that the Spirit of the Lord rests upon them.

We believe that skillful and godly wisdom has entered into the heart of our president and knowledge is pleasant to him. Discretion watches over him; understanding keeps him and delivers him from the way of evil and from evil men.

Father, we ask that You compass the president about with men and women who make their hearts and ears attentive to godly counsel and do that which is right in Your sight. We believe You cause them to be men and women of integrity who are obedient concerning us that we may lead a quiet and peaceable life in all godliness and honesty. We pray that the upright shall dwell in our government... that men and women blameless and complete in Your sight, Father, shall remain in these positions of authority; but the wicked shall be cut off our government and the treacherous shall be rooted out of it.

Your Word declares that **blessed is the nation whose God is the Lord** (Ps. 33:12). We receive Your blessing. Father, you are our refuge and stronghold in times of trouble (high cost, destitution, and desperation). So we declare with our mouths that Your people dwell safely in this land, and we *prosper* abundantly. We are more than conquerors through Christ Jesus!

It is written in Your Word that the heart of the king is in the hand of the Lord, and you turn it whichever way you desire. We believe the heart of our leader is in Your hand and that his decisions are divinely directed of the lord.

We give thanks unto You that the good news of the Gospel is published in our land. The Word of the lord prevails and grows mightily in the hearts and lives of the people. We give thanks for this land and the leaders You have given to us, in Jesus' name.

Jesus is Lord over the United States!

Scripture References

1 Timothy 2:1-3	Deuteronomy 28:10,11
Proverbs 2:10-12 AMP	Romans 8:37
Proverbs 2:21,22 AMP	Proverbs 21:1
Psalm 33:12	Acts 12:24
Psalm 9:9	

38
School Systems and Children

Father, we thank You that the entrance of Your Word brings light and thank You that You watch over Your Word to perform it. Father, we bring before You the _____ school system(s) and the men and women who are in positions of authority within the school system(s).

We believe that skillful and godly wisdom has entered into their hearts; that Your knowledge is pleasant to them. Discretion watches over them; understanding keeps them and delivers them from the way of evil and from evil men. We pray that men and women of integrity, blameless, and complete in Your sight, remain in these positions, but that the wicked be cut off and the treacherous be rooted out in the name of Jesus. Father, we thank You for born-again, Spirit-filled people in these positions.

Father, we bring our children, our young people before You. We speak forth Your Word boldly and confidently, Father, that we and our households are saved in the name of Jesus. We are redeemed from the curse of the law for Jesus was made a curse for us. *Our sons and daughters are not given to another people.* We enjoy our children, and they shall not go into captivity, in the name of Jesus.

As parents, we train our children in the way they should go, and when they are old they shall not depart from it.

Our children shrink from whatever might offend You, Father, and discredit the name of Christ. They show themselves to be blameless, guileless, innocent, and uncontaminated children of God without blemish (faultless, unrebukable) in the midst of a crooked and wicked generation, holding out to it and offering to all the Word of Life. Thank You, Father, that You give them knowledge and skill in all learning and wisdom, and bring them into favor with those around them.

Father, we pray and intercede that these young people, their parents, and the leaders in the school system(s) separate themselves from contact with contaminating and corrupting influences. They cleanse themselves from everything that would contaminate and defile their spirits, souls, and bodies.

We confess that they shun immorality and all sexual looseness — flee from impurity in thought, word or deed. They live and conduct themselves honorably and becomingly as in the open light of day. We confess and believe that they shun youthful lusts and flee from them in the name of Jesus.

Satan, we speak to you in the name of Jesus. We bind you, the principalities, the powers, the rulers of the darkness, and wicked spirits in heavenly places and tear down strongholds using the mighty weapons God has provided for us in the name of Jesus. We bind up that binding spirit of antichrist. We bind every spirit of the occult — astrology, witchcraft, every familiar spirit. We bind sexual immorality, idolatry, obscenity, and profanity. We bind those spirits of alcohol, nicotine, and drug addiction. We bind worldly wisdom in any form — every opposer to the truth. We bind every destructive, deceitful, thieving spirit. You are loosed from your assignment against _____ in the name of Jesus for they escape from the snare of the devil who has held them captive.

We commission the ministering spirits to go forth and police the area dispelling the forces of darkness.

Father, we thank You that in Christ all the treasures of divine wisdom (of comprehensive insight into the ways and purposes of God) and all the riches of spiritual knowledge and enlightenment are stored up and lie hidden for us, and we walk in Him.

We praise You, Father, that we shall see _____ walking in the ways of piety and virtue, revering Your name, Father. Those who err in spirit will come to understanding and those who murmur discontentedly will accept instruction in the Way, Jesus, to Your will and carry out Your purposes in their lives, for You, Father, occupy first place in their hearts. We surround _____ with our faith.

Thank You, Father, that You are the delivering God. Thank You, that the good news of the Gospel is published throughout our school system(s). Thank You, for intercessors to stand on Your Word and for laborers of the harvest to preach Your Word in Jesus' name. Praise the Lord!

Scripture References

Psalm 119:130
Jeremiah 1:12
Proverbs 2:10-12 AMP
Proverbs 2:21,22 AMP
Acts 16:31
Galatians 3:13
Deuteronomy 28:32,41
Proverbs 22:6 AMP
Philippians 2:15,16 AMP
Daniel 1:17 AMP
Daniel 1:9
1 John 2:17 AMP

2 Timothy 2:21 AMP
2 Corinthians 7:1 AMP
1 Corinthians 6:18 AMP
Romans 13:13 AMP
Ephesians 5:4
2 Timothy 2:22
Matthew 18:18
2 Timothy 2:26
Hebrews 1:14
Colossians 2:3 AMP
Isaiah 29:23,24 AMP

39
Adoration
"Hallowed Be Thy Name"

Our Father, which art in heaven, hallowed be Thy name.

Bless the lord, O my soul: and all that is within me, bless Your Holy name. I adore You and make known to You my adoration and love this day.

I bless Your name, *Elohim,* the Creator of heaven and earth, Who was in the beginning. It is You Who made me, and You have crowned me with glory and honor. You are the God of might and strength. Hallowed be Thy name!

I bless Your name, *El-Shaddai,* the God Almighty of Blessings. You are the Breasty One Who nourishes and supplies. You are All-Bountiful and All-Sufficient. Hallowed be Thy name!

I bless Your name, *Adonai,* my Lord and my Master. You are Jehovah — the Completely Self-Existing One, always present, revealed in Jesus Who is the same yesterday, today and forever. Hallowed be Thy name!

I bless Your name, *Jehovah-Jireh,* the One Who sees my needs and provides for them. Hallowed be Thy name!

I bless Your name, *Jehovah-Rapha,* my Healer and the One Who makes bitter experiences sweet. You sent Your Word and healed me. You forgave all my iniquities and You healed all my diseases. Hallowed be Thy name!

I bless Your name, *Jehovah-M'Kaddesh,* the Lord my Sanctifier. You have set me apart for Yourself. Hallowed be Thy name!

Jehovah-Nissi, You are my Victory, my Banner, and my Standard. Your banner over me is love. When the enemy shall come in like a flood, You will lift up a standard against him. Hallowed be Thy name!

Jehovah-Shalom, I bless Your name. You are my Peace — the peace which transcends all understanding, which garrisons and mounts guard over my heart and mind in Christ Jesus. Hallowed be Thy name!

I bless You, *Jehovah-Tsidkenu,* my Righteousness. Thank You for becoming sin for me that I might become the righteousness of God in Christ Jesus. Hallowed be Thy name!

Jehovah-Rohi, You are my Shepherd and I shall not want for any good or beneficial thing. Hallowed be Thy name!

Hallelujah to *Jehovah-Shammah* Who will never leave or forsake me. You are always there. I take comfort and am encouraged and confidently and boldly say, The Lord is my Helper, I will not be seized with alarm — I will not fear or dread or be terrorized. What can man do to me? Hallowed be Thy name!

I worship and adore You, *El-Elyon,* the Most High God Who is the First Cause of everything, the Possessor of the heavens and earth. You are the Everlasting-God, the Great-God, the Living-God, the Merciful-God. You are Truth, Justice, Righteousness, and Perfection. You are *El-Elyon* — the Highest Sovereign of the heavens and the earth. Hallowed be Thy name!

Father, You have exalted above all else Your name and Your Word, and You have magnified Your Word above all Your name! The Word was made flesh, and dwelt among us, and His name is JESUS! Hallowed be Thy name!

Scripture References

Matthew 6:9
Psalm 103:1
Genesis 1:1,2
Psalm 8:5b
Genesis 49:24,25
Genesis 15:1,2,8
Hebrews 13:8
Genesis 22:14
Psalm 147:3 AMP
Exodus 15:23-26 AMP
Psalm 107:20
Psalm 103:3
Leviticus 20:7,8
Exodus 17:15
Song of Solomon 2:4
Isaiah 59:19
Judges 6:24
Philippians 4:7 AMP
Jeremiah 23:5,6
2 Corinthians 5:21
Psalm 23:1
Psalm 34:10
Ezekiel 48:35
Hebrews 13:5
Hebrews 13:6 AMP
Psalm 91:1
Psalm 138:2 AMP
John 1:14

40
Divine Intervention
"Thy Kingdom Come"

Father, I pray according to Matthew 6:10, Thy Kingdom come. I am looking for the soon coming of our Lord and Savior Jesus Christ.

Today, we are [even here and] now Your children; it is not yet disclosed (made clear) what we shall be [hereafter], *but we know that when He comes and is manifested we shall [as God's children] resemble and be like Him, for we shall see Him just as He [really] is.* You said that everyone who has this hope [resting] on Him cleanses (purifies) himself just as He is pure — chaste, undefiled, guiltless.

For the grace of God — His unmerited favor and blessing — has come forward (appeared) for the deliverance from sin and the eternal salvation for all mankind. It has trained us to reject and renounce all ungodliness (irreligion) and worldly (passionate) desires, to live discreet (temperate, self-controlled), upright, devout (spiritually whole) lives in this present world, awaiting and looking for the [fulfillment, the realization of our] blessed hope, *even the glorious appearing of our great God and Savior Christ Jesus, the Messiah, the Anointed One.*

For the Lord Himself shall descent from heaven with a shout, with the voice of the archangel, and with the trump of God: and the dead in Christ shall rise first. Then we which are alive and remain shall be caught up together with them in the clouds, to meet the Lord in the air: and so shall we ever be with the Lord.

I thank You, Father, that the Lord shall come (to earth), and all the holy ones [saints and angels] with Him; and the Lord shall be King over all the earth; in that day He shall be one Lord, and His name one. The government shall be upon His shoulder.

Father, I thank You that we shall join the great voices in heaven saying, The Kingdoms of this world are become the kingdoms of our Lord, and of His Christ; and He shall reign for ever and ever.

Yours, O Lord, is the greatness, and power, and the glory, and the victory, and the majesty; for all that is in the heavens and the earth is Yours; Yours is the Kingdom, O Lord, and Yours it is to be exalted as head over all. Thy Kingdom come. Hallelujah!

Scripture References

1 John 3:2,3 AMP
Titus 2:11-13 AMP
1 Thessalonians 4:16,17
Zechariah 14:5,9 AMP

Isaiah 9:6 AMP
Revelation 11:15
1 Chronicles 29:11 AMP

41
Submission
"Thy Will Be Done"

Father, I pray that the will of God be done in my life as it is in heaven. For I am Your [own] handiwork (Your workmanship), recreated in Christ Jesus, [born anew] that I may do those good works which You predestined (planned beforehand) for me, (taking paths which You prepared ahead of time) that I should walk in them — living the good life which You prearranged and made ready for me to live.

Teach me to do Your Will, for You are my God; let Your good Spirit lead me into a plain country and into the land of uprightness. Jesus, You gave (yielded) Yourself up [to atone] for my sins (and to save and sanctify me), in order to rescue and deliver me from this present wicked age and world order, in accordance with the will and purpose and plan of our God and Father.

In the name of Jesus, I am not conformed to this world, but am transformed by the renewing of my mind, that I may prove what is that good, and acceptable, and perfect, will of God. For this is the will of God, that I should be consecrated — separated and set apart for pure and holy living; that I should abstain from all sexual vice; that I should know how to possess [control, manage] my own body (in purity, separated from things profane, and) in consecration and honor, not [to be used] in the passion of lust, like the heathen who are ignorant of the true God and have no knowledge of His will.

Father, thank You that You chose me — actually picked me out for Yourself as Your own — in Christ before the foundation of the world; that I should be holy (consecrated and set apart for You) and blameless in Your sight, even above reproach, before You in love: having predestinated me unto the adoption of a child by Jesus Christ to Yourself, according to the good pleasure of Your will.

Your will be done on earth in my life as it is in heaven. Amen and so be it!

Scripture References

Matthew 6:9b,10
Ephesians 2:10 AMP
Psalm 143:10 AMP
Galatians 1:4 AMP

Romans 12:2
1 Thessalonians 4:4,5 AMP
Ephesians 1:4 AMP
Ephesians 1:5

42

Provision
"Give Us This Day Our Daily Bread"

In the name of Jesus, I confess with the Psalmist David, I have not seen the righteous forsaken, nor his seed begging bread.

Father, thank You for food, clothing and shelter. In the name of Jesus, I have stopped being perpetually uneasy (anxious and worried) about my life, what I shall eat and what I shall drink, or about my body, what I shall put on. My life is greater [in quality] than food, and the body [far above and more excellent] than clothing.

The bread of idleness [gossip, discontent and self-pity] I will not eat. It is You, Father, Who will liberally supply (fill to the full) my every need according to Your riches in glory in Christ Jesus.

In the name of Jesus, I shall not live by bread alone, but by every word that proceeds from the mouth of God. Your words were found, and I did eat them, and Your Word was to me a joy and the rejoicing of my heart.

And the Word became flesh, and dwelt among us. Jesus, You are the Bread of Life; You give me life, the Living Bread.

Thank You, Father, in the name of Jesus, for spiritual bread — manna from heaven.

Prayers to the Father

Scripture References

Matthew 6:9b-11
Psalm 37:25
Matthew 6:25 AMP
Proverbs 31:27b AMP
Philippians 4:19 AMP

Matthew 4:4
Jeremiah 15:16 AMP
John 1:14a
John 6:48-51 AMP

43

Forgiveness
"Forgive Us Our Debts"

Father, I forgive everyone who has trespassed against me so that You can forgive me my trespasses. [Now, having received the Holy Spirit and being led and directed by Him] if I forgive the sins of anyone they are forgiven; if I retain the sins of anyone, they are retained.

Father, Your Word says, **Love your enemies and pray for those who persecute you** (Matt. 5:44 AMP). I come before you in Jesus' name to lift _____ before You. I invoke blessings upon him/her and pray for his/her happiness. I implore Your blessings (favor) upon him/her.

Father, not only will I pray for _____, but I set myself to treat him/her well (do good to, act nobly toward) him/her. I will be merciful, sympathetic, tender, responsive, and compassionate toward _____ even as You are, Father. I am an imitator of You, and I can do all things through Christ Jesus Who strengthens me.

Father, I thank You that I have great peace in this situation, for I love Your law and refuse to take offense toward _____.

Jesus, I am blessed — happy [with life — joy and satisfaction in God's favor and salvation apart from outward conditions] and to be envied — because I take no offense in You and refuse to be hurt or resentful or annoyed or repelled or made to stumble, [whatever may occur].

And now, Father, I roll this work upon You — commit and trust it wholly to You; and believe that You will cause my thoughts to become in agreement to Your will, and so my plans shall be established and succeed.

Scripture References

Matthew 6:12
Matthew 6:14,15
John 20:23 AMP
Luke 6:27b AMP
Matthew 5:44 AMP
Luke 6:28 AMP

Ephesians 5:1 AMP
Philippians 4:13 AMP
Psalm 119:165 AMP
Luke 7:23 AMP
Proverbs 16:3 AMP

44
Guidance and Deliverance
"Lead Us Not Into Temptation"

There has no temptation taken me but such as is common to man: but *God is faithful,* Who will not suffer me to be tempted above that which I am able; but will with the temptation also make a way to escape, that I may be able to bear it.

I count it all joy when I fall into various temptations; knowing this, that the trying of my faith works patience.

I will not say when I am tempted, I am tempted from God; for God is incapable of being tempted by [what is] evil and He himself tempts no one.

Thank You, Jesus, for giving Yourself for my sins, that You might deliver me from this present evil world, according to the will of God and our Father: to Whom be glory for ever and ever.

Father, in the name of Jesus, and according to the power that is at work in me, I will keep awake (give strict attention, be cautious) and watch and pray that I may not come into temptation. In Jesus' name, amen.

Scripture References

1 Corinthians 10:13 Galatians 1:4,5
James 1:2,3 Ephesians 3:20b
James 1:13 AMP Matthew 26:41a AMP

45

Praise
"For Thine Is the Kingdom and the Power, and the Glory"

O magnify the Lord with me, and let us exalt His name together.

As for God, His way is perfect! The Word of the Lord is tested and tried; He is a shield to all those who take refuge and put their trust in Him.

Let the words of my mouth and the meditation of my heart be acceptable in Your sight, O Lord, my firm, impenetrable Rock and my Redeemer.

Your Word has revived me and given me life.

Forever, O Lord, Your Word is settled in heaven.

Your Word is a lamp to my feet and a light to my path.

The sum of Your Word is truth and every one of Your righteous decrees endures forever.

I will worship toward Your holy temple, and praise Your name for Your loving-kindness and for Your truth and faithfulness; for You have exalted above all else Your name and Your Word, and You have magnified Your Word above all Your name!

Let my prayer be set forth as incense before You, the lifting up of my hands as the evening sacrifice. Set a guard, O Lord, before my mouth; keep watch at the door of my lips.

Praise

He who brings an offering of praise and thanksgiving honors and glorifies Me; and he who orders his way aright — who prepares the way that I may show him — to him I will demonstrate the salvation of God.

My mouth shall be filled with your praise and with your honor all the day.

Because Your loving-kindness is better than life, my lips shall praise You. So will I bless You while I live; I will lift up my hands in Your name.

Your testimonies also are my delight and my counselors.

Scripture References (AMP)

Psalm 34:3	Psalm 138:2
Psalm 18:30	Psalm 141:2,3
Psalm 19:14	Psalm 50:23
Psalm 119:50	Psalm 71:8
Psalm 119:89	Psalm 63:3,4
Psalm 119:105	Psalm 119:24
Psalm 119:160	

46
Victory Over Pride

Father, Your Word says that You hate a proud look, that You resist the proud but give grace to the humble. I submit myself therefore to You, God. In the name of Jesus, I resist the devil, and he will flee from me. I renounce every manifestation of pride in my life as sin; I repent and turn from it.

As an act of faith, I clothe myself with humility and receive Your grace. I humble myself under Your mighty hand, Lord, that You may exalt me in due time. I refuse to exalt myself. I do not think of myself more highly than I ought; I do not have an exaggerated opinion of my own importance, but rate my ability with sober judgment, according to the degree of faith apportioned to me.

Proverbs 11:2 says, When pride cometh, then cometh shame: but with the lowly is wisdom. Father, I set myself to resist pride when it comes. My desire is to be counted among the lowly, so I take on the attitude of a servant.

Father, thank You that You dwell with him who is of a contrite and humble spirit. You revive the spirit of the humble and revive the heart of the contrite ones. Thank You that the reward of humility and the reverent and worshipful fear of the Lord is riches and honor and life.

Scripture References

Proverbs 6:16	Proverbs 11:2
James 4:6,7	Matthew 23:11
Proverbs 21:4	Isaiah 57:15
1 Peter 5:5,6	Proverbs 22:4 AMP
Romans 12:3 AMP	

47
Victory Over Fear

Father, in Jesus' name, I confess and believe that no weapon formed against me shall prosper, and any tongue that rises against me in judgment I shall show to be in the wrong. I believe I dwell in the secret place of the Most High. I shall remain stable and fixed under the shadow of the Almighty God whose power no foe can withstand — this secret place hides me from the strife of tongues.

I believe the wisdom of God's Word dwells in me, and because it does, I realize that I am without fear or dread of evil. In all my ways I know and acknowledge God and His Word; thus, He directs and makes straight and plain my pathway. As I attend to God's Word, it is health to my nerves and sinews, and marrow and moistening to my bones.

I am strengthened and reinforced with mighty power in my innerself by the Holy Spirit Himself Who dwells in me. God is my strength and my refuge, and I confidently trust in Him and in His Word. I am empowered through my union with Almighty God. This gives me the superhuman, supernatural strength to walk in divine health and to live in abundance.

God Himself has said, **I will never leave you without support or forsake you or let you down, my child. [I will] not, [I will] not, [I will] not in any degree leave you helpless or relax my hold on you... assuredly not!** (Heb. 13:5 AMP)

I take comfort and am encouraged and confidently and boldly say, "The Lord is my helper. I will not be seized with alarm. I will not fear or be terrified, for what can man do to me?"

I confess and believe that my children are disciples taught of the Lord and obedient o God's will. Great is the peace and undisturbed composure of my children — because God Himself contends with that which contends with me and my children, and He gives them safety and eases them. God will perfect that which concerns me.

This Word of God that I have spoken is alive and full of power. It is active and operative. It energizes me, and it affects me. As I speak God's Word, it is sharper than any two-edged sword, and it is penetrating into my joints and into the marrow of my bones. It is healing to my flesh. It is prosperity for me. It is the magnificent Word of Almighty God. According to His Word that I have spoken, so be it! Hallelujah!

Scripture References

Isaiah 54:17 AMP	Ephesians 6:10 AMP
Psalm 91:1 AMP	Hebrews 13:5,6 AMP
Psalm 31:20	Isaiah 54:13 AMP
Proverbs 3:6,8 AMP	Isaiah 49:25 AMP
Ephesians 3:16 AMP	Psalm 138:8 AMP
Psalm 91:2	Hebrews 4:12 AMP

48
Victory Over Depression

Father, You are my refuge and my high tower and my stronghold in times of trouble. I lean on and confidently put my trust in You, for You have not forsaken me. I seek You on the authority of Your Word and the right of my necessity. I praise You, the help of my countenance and my God.

Lord, You lift up those who are bowed down. Therefore, I am strong and my heart takes courage. I establish myself on righteousness — right standing in conformity with Your will and order. I am far even from the thought of oppression or destruction, for I fear not. I am far from terror, for it shall not come near me.

Father, You have thoughts and plans for my welfare and peace. *My mind is stayed on You,* for I stop allowing myself to be agitated and disturbed and intimidated and cowardly and unsettled.

Satan, I resist you and every oppressive spirit in the name of Jesus. I resist fear, discouragement, self-pity, and depression. I speak the Word of truth, in the power of God, and I give you no place, Satan; I give no opportunity to you. I am delivered from oppression by the Blood of the Lamb.

Father, I thank You that I have been given a spirit of power and of love and of a calm and well-balanced mind. I have discipline and self-control.

I have the mind of Christ and hold the thoughts, feelings, and purposes of His heart.

I have a fresh mental and spiritual attitude, for I am constantly renewed in the spirit of my mind with Your Word, Father.

Therefore, I brace up and reinvigorate and cut through and make firm and straight paths for my feet — safe and upright and happy paths that go in the right direction.

I arise from the depression and prostration in which circumstances have kept me. I rise to new life, I shine and am radiant with the glory of the Lord.

Thank You, Father, in Jesus' name that I am set free from every evil work.

I praise You that the joy of the Lord is my strength and stronghold! Hallelujah!

Scripture References

Psalm 9:9,10 AMP
Psalm 146:8
Psalm 31:24 AMP
Isaiah 35:3,4
Isaiah 54:14
Isaiah 50:10
Jeremiah 29:11-13 AMP
Isaiah 26:3
John 14:27 AMP
James 4:7

Ephesians 4:27
Luke 4:18,19
2 Timothy 1:7 AMP
1 Corinthians 2:16 AMP
Philippians 2:5
Ephesians 4:23,24 AMP
Hebrews 12:12,13 AMP
Isaiah 60:1 AMP
Galatians 1:4
Nehemiah 8:10 AMP

49
Victory Over Gluttony

Father, it is written in Your Word that if I confess with my lips that Jesus is Lord and believe in my heart that You have raised Him from the dead, I shall be saved. Father, I am Your child and confess that Jesus Christ is Lord over my spirit, my soul, and my body. I make Him Lord over every situation in my life. Therefore, I can do all things through Christ Jesus who strengthens me.

Father, *I have made a quality decision to give You my appetite*. I choose Jesus rather than the indulgence of my flesh. I command my body to get in line with Your Word. I eat only as much as is sufficient for me. I eat and am satisfied.

When I sit down to eat, I consider what is before me. I am not given to the desire of dainties or deceitful foods.

Like a boxer, I buffet my body — handle it roughly, discipline it by hardships — and subdue it. I bring my body into subjection to my spirit man — the inward man — the real me. Not all things are helpful — good for me to do though permissible. I will not become the slave of anything or be brought under its power.

My body is for the Lord. I dedicate my body — presenting all my members and faculties — as a living sacrifice, holy and well pleasing to You, presenting them as implements of righteousness. I am united to You, Lord, and become one spirit with You. My body is the temple, the very sanctuary, of the Holy Spirit who lives within me, whom I have received as a gift from You, Father.

Prayers for Victory

I am not my own. I was bought for a price, made Your own. So then, I honor You and bring glory to You in my body. Therefore, I always exercise and discipline myself, bringing under authority my carnal affections, bodily appetites, and worldly desires. I endeavor in all respects to have a clean conscience, void of offense toward You, Father, and toward men. I keep myself from idols — from anything and everything that would occupy the place in my heart due to You, from any sort of substitute for You that would take first place in my life.

I no longer spend the rest of my natural life living by my human appetites and desires, but I live for what You will! I am on my guard. I refuse to be overburdened and depressed, weighed down with the giddiness and headache and nausea of self-indulgence, drunkenness (one food), worldly worries and cares, for I have been given a spirit of power and of love and of a sound mind. I have discipline and self-control.

Father, I *do* resist temptation in the name of Jesus. I strip off and throw aside every encumbrance — unnecessary weight — and this gluttony which so readily tries to cling to and entangle me. I run with patient endurance and steady persistence the appointed course of the race that is set before me, looking away from all distractions to Jesus, the author and finisher of my faith.

Christ the Messiah *will* be magnified and get glory and praise in this body of mine and *will* be boldly exalted in my person. Thank You, Father, in Jesus' name! Hallelujah!

Scripture References

Romans 10:9,10	Romans 12:1 AMP
Philippians 4:13	1 Corinthians 6:19,20 AMP
Deuteronomy 30:19	Luke 21:34 AMP
Proverbs 25:16	2 Timothy 1:7 AMP
Proverbs 23:1-3	James 4:7
1 Corinthians 9:27 AMP	Hebrews 12:1,2
1 Corinthians 6:12,13,17 AMP	Philippians 1:20

50
Victory in Court Cases

Father, in the name of Jesus, it is written in Your Word to call on You and You will answer me and show me great and mighty things. I put You in remembrance of Your Word and thank You that You watch over it to perform it.

I say that no weapon formed against me shall prosper and any tongue that rises against me in judgment I shall show to be in the wrong.

This peace, security, and triumph over opposition is my inheritance as Your child. This is the righteousness which I obtain from You, Father, which You impart to me as my justification.

I am far from even the thought of destruction, for I shall not fear and terror shall not come near me.

Father, You say You will establish me to the end — keep me steadfast, give me strength, and guarantee my vindication; that is, be my warrant against all accusation or indictment.

Father, You contend with those who contend with me, and You perfect that which concerns me. I dwell in the secret place of the Most High, and this secret place hides me from the strife of tongues, for a false witness who breathes out lies is an abomination to You.

I am a true witness and all my words are upright and in right standing with You, Father. By my long forbearing and calmness of spirit the judge is persuaded, and my soft speech breaks down the most bondlike resistance.

Prayers for Victory

Therefore, I am not anxious beforehand how I shall reply in defense or what I am to say, for the Holy Spirit teaches me *in that very hour* and moment what I ought to say to those in the outside world. My speech is seasoned with salt.

I thank You, Father, that Satan and all menacing spirits are bound from operating against me, for I am strong in You, Lord, and in the power of Your might. Your shield of faith quenches every fiery dart.

Thank You, Father, that I increase in wisdom and in stature and years, and in *favor* with You, God, and man. Praise the Lord!

Scripture References

Jeremiah 33:3
Jeremiah 1:12 AMP
Isaiah 43:26 AMP
Isaiah 54:17 AMP
Isaiah 54:14 AMP
1 Corinthians 1:8 AMP
Isaiah 49:25
Psalm 138:8
Psalm 91:1
Psalm 31:20

Proverbs 6:19
Proverbs 14:25
Proverbs 8:8 AMP
Proverbs 25:15
Luke 12:11,12 AMP
Colossians 4:6
Matthew 18:18
Ephesians 6:10,16
Luke 2:52 AMP

Part II
What the Word Says

Being a Father Who Is Godly

Let this mind be in you, which was also in Christ Jesus.

Who, being in the form of God, thought it not robbery to be equal with God.

But made himself of no reputation, and took upon him the form of a servant, and was made in the likeness of men:

And being found in fashion as a man, he humbled himself, and became obedient unto death, even the death of the cross.

Philippians 2:5-8

He that walketh with wise men shall be wise: but a companion of fools shall be destroyed.

Proverbs 13:20

Verily, verily, I say unto you, The servant is not greater than his lord; neither he that is sent greater than he that sent him.

A new commandment I give unto you, That ye love one another; as I have loved you, that ye also love one another.

John 13:16,34

Moreover it is required in stewards, that a man be found faithful.

1 Corinthians 4:2

Therefore, my beloved brethren, be ye stedfast, unmoveable, always abounding in the work of the Lord, forasmuch as ye know that your labour is not in vain in the Lord.

1 Corinthians 15:58

Bear ye one another's burdens, and so fulfill the law of Christ.

As we have therefore opportunity, let us do good unto all men, especially unto them who are of the household of faith.

Galatians 6:2,10

Be ye therefore followers of God, as dear children;

And walk in love, as Christ also hath loved us, and hath given himself for us an offering and a sacrifice to God for a sweetsmelling savour.

Ephesians 5:1,2

Forbearing one another, and forgiving one another, if any man have a quarrel against any: even as Christ forgave you, so also do ye.

Servants, obey in all things your masters according to the flesh; not with eyeservice, as menpleasers; but in singleness of heart, fearing God.

Colossians 3:13,22

Being a Father Who Is Loving

Though I speak with the tongues of men and of angels, and have not charity, I am become as sounding brass, or a tinkling cymbal.

And though I have the gift of prophecy, and understand all mysteries, and all knowledge; and though I have all faith, so that I could remove mountains, and have not charity, I am nothing.

And though I bestow all my goods to feed the poor, and though I give my body to be burned, and have not charity, it profiteth me nothing.

Charity suffereth long, and is kind; charity envieth not; charity vaunteth not itself, is not puffed up,

Doth not behave itself unseemly, seeketh not her own, is not easily provoked, thinketh no evil;

Rejoiceth not in iniquity, but rejoiceth in the truth;

Beareth all things, believeth all things, hopeth all things, endureth all things.

Charity never faileth.

1 Corinthians 13:1-8a

Owe no man any thing, but to love one another: for he that loveth another hath fulfilled the law.

Love worketh no ill to his neighbour: therefore love is the fulfilling of the law.

Romans 13:8,10

And now abideth faith, hope, charity, these three; but the greatest of these is charity.

1 Corinthians 13:13

For this is the message that ye heard from the beginning, that we should love one another.

We know that we have passed from death unto life, because we love the brethren. He that loveth not his brother abideth in death.

My little children, let us not love in word, neither in tongue; but in deed and in truth.

1 John 3:11,14,18

Beloved, let us love one another: for love is of God; and every one that loveth is born of God, and knoweth God.

He that loveth not knoweth not God; for God is love.

1 John 4:7,8

Hatred stirreth up strifes: but love covereth all sins.

Proverbs 10:12

Give to him that asketh thee, and from him that would borrow of thee turn not thou away.

Matthew 5:42

Being a Father Who Is Giving

But this I say, He which soweth sparingly shall reap also sparingly; and he which soweth bountifully shall reap also bountifully.

Every man according as he purposeth in his heart, so let him give; not grudgingly, or of necessity: for God loveth a cheerful giver.

And God is able to make all grace abound toward you; that ye, always having all sufficiency in all things, may abound to every good work.

2 Corinthians 9:6-8

Cease from anger, and forsake wrath: fret not thyself in any wise to do evil.

Psalm 37:8

A good man sheweth favour, and lendeth: he will guide his affairs with discretion.

Psalm 112:5

A friend loveth at all times, and a brother is born for adversity.

Proverbs 17:17

He that hath pity upon the poor lendeth unto the Lord; and that which he hath given will he pay him again.

Proverbs 19:17

He that hath a bountiful eye shall be blessed; for he giveth of his bread to the poor.

Proverbs 22:9

He that giveth unto the poor shall not lack; but he that hideth his eyes shall have many a curse.

Proverbs 28:27

Therefore all things whatsoever ye would that men should do to you, do ye even so to them: for this is the law and the prophets.

Matthew 7:12

Give, and it shall be given unto you; good measure, pressed down, and shaken together, and running over, shall men give into your bosom. For with the same measure that ye mete withal it shall be measured to you again.

Luke 6:38

Upon the first day of the week let every one of you lay by him in store, as God hath prospered him, that there be no gatherings when I come.

1 Corinthians 16:2

Being a Father Who Listens

But be ye doers of the word, and not hearers only, deceiving your own selves.

For if any be a hearer of the word, and not a doer, he is like unto a man beholding his natural face in a glass:

But whoso looketh into the perfect law of liberty, and continueth therein, he being not a forgetful hearer, but a doer of the work, this man shall be blessed in his deed.

James 1:22,23,25

He that hath an ear, let him hear what the Spirit saith unto the churches.

Revelation 2:29

The heart of the prudent getteth knowledge; and the ear of the wise seeketh knowledge.

Proverbs 18:15

And the man said unto me, Son of man, behold with thine eyes, and hear with thine ears, and set thine heart upon all that I shall shew thee.

Ezekiel 40:4a

And every one that heareth these sayings of mine, and doeth them not, shall be likened unto a foolish man, which built his house upon the sand:

And the rain descended, and the floods came, and the winds blew, and beat upon that house; and it fell: and great was the fall of it.

Matthew 7:26,27

But blessed are your eyes, for they see: and your ears, for they hear.

Matthew 13:16

Take heed therefore how ye hear: for whosoever hath, to him shall be given; and whosoever hath not, from him shall be taken even that which he seemeth to have.

Luke 8:18

He that is of God heareth God's words: ye therefore hear them not, because ye are not of God.

John 8:47

Pilate therefore said unto him, Art thou a king then? Jesus answered, Thou sayest that I am a king. To this end was I born, and for this cause came I into the world, that I should bear witness unto the truth. Every one that is of the truth heareth my voice.

John 18:37

Being a Father Who Is Patient

And not only so, but we glory in tribulations also: knowing that tribulation worketh patience.

And patience, experience; and experience, hope:

And hope maketh not ashamed; because the love of God is shed abroad in our hearts by the Holy Ghost which is given unto us.

Romans 5:3-5

I can do all things through Christ which strengtheneth me.

Philippians 4:13

Knowing this, that the trying of your faith worketh patience.

But let patience have her perfect work, that ye may be perfect and entire, wanting nothing.

James 1:3,4

Be ye strong therefore, and let not your hands be weak: for your work shall be rewarded.

2 Chronicles 15:7

Wait on the Lord: be of good courage, and he shall strengthen thine heart; wait, I say, on the Lord.

Psalm 27:14

Rest in the Lord, and wait patiently for him: fret not thyself because of him who prospereth in his way, because of the man who bringeth wicked devices to pass.

Psalm 37:7

I waited patiently for the Lord; and he inclined unto me, and heard my cry.

Psalm 40:1

For thou art my hope, O Lord God: thou art my trust from my youth.

Psalm 71:5

Better is the end of a thing than the beginning thereof: and the patient in spirit is better than the proud in spirit.

Be not hasty in thy spirit to be angry: for anger resteth in the bosom of fools.

Ecclesiastes 7:8,9

But they that wait upon the Lord shall renew their strength; they shall mount up with wings as eagles; they shall run, and not be weary; and they shall walk, and not faint.

Isaiah 40:31

In your patience possess ye your souls.

Luke 21:19

Being a Father Who Is Knowledgeable

Now therefore go, and I will be with thy mouth, and teach thee what thou shalt say.

Exodus 4:12

Teach me, and I will hold my tongue: and cause me to understand wherein I have erred.

Job 6:24

Shew me thy ways, O Lord; teach me thy paths.

Lead me in thy truth, and teach me: for thou art the God of my salvation; on thee do I wait all the day.

The meek will he guide in judgment: and the meek will he teach his way.

What man is he that feareth the Lord? him shall he teach in the way that he shall choose.

Psalm 25:4,5,9,12

Teach me thy way, O Lord, and lead me in a plain path, because of mine enemies.

Psalm 27:11

I will instruct thee and teach thee in the way which thou shalt go: I will guide thee with mine eye.

Psalm 32:8

I have declared my ways, and thou heardest me: teach me thy statutes.

Make me to understand the way of thy precepts: so shall I talk of thy wondrous works.

Psalm 119:26,27

Teach me to do thy will; for thou art my God: thy spirit is good; lead me into the land of uprightness.

Psalm 143:10

He that walketh with wise men shall be wise: but a companion of fools shall be destroyed.

Proverbs 13:20

When the scorner is punished, the simple is made wise: and when the wise is instructed, he receiveth knowledge.

Proverbs 21:11

O Lord, I know that the way of man is not in himself: it is not in man that walketh to direct his steps.

Jeremiah 10:23

Call unto me, and I will answer thee, and shew thee great and mighty things, which thou knowest not.

Jeremiah 33:3

Being a Father Who Is Honorable

Finally, brethren, whatsoever things are true, whatsoever things are honest, whatsoever things are just, whatsoever things are pure, whatsoever things are lovely, whatsoever things are of good report; if there be any virtue, and if there be any praise, think on these things.

Philippians 4:8

Let me be weighed in an even balance, that God may know mine integrity.

Job 31:6

Blessed is the man that walketh not in the counsel of the ungodly, nor standeth in the way of sinners, nor sitteth in the seat of the scornful.

But his delight is in the law of the Lord; and in his law doth he meditate day and night.

Psalm 1:1,2

Judge me, O Lord; for I have walked in mine integrity: I have trusted also in the Lord; therefore I shall not slide.

Psalm 26:1

All the paths of the Lord are mercy and truth unto such as keep his covenant and his testimonies.

Let integrity and uprightness preserve me; for I wait on thee.

Psalm 25:10,21

And as for me, thou upholdest me in mine integrity, and settest me before thy face for ever.

Psalm 41:12

So he fed them according to the integrity of his heart; and guided them by the skilfulness of his hands.

Psalm 78:72

The fear of the Lord is the beginning of wisdom: a good understanding have all they that do his commandments: his praise endureth for ever.

Psalm 111:10

Blessed are they that keep his testimonies, and that seek him with the whole heart.

Thou hast commanded us to keep thy precepts diligently.

Psalm 119:2,4

The integrity of the upright shall guide them: but the perverseness of transgressors shall destroy them.

Proverbs 11:3

Being a Father Who Is a Leader

The steps of a good man are ordered by the Lord: and he delighteth in his way.

Psalm 37:23

For the Lord God is a sun and shield: the Lord will give grace and glory: no good thing will he withhold from them that walk uprightly.

Psalm 84:11

A good man sheweth favour, and lendeth: he will guide his affairs with discretion.

Psalm 112:5

Better is a little with righteousness than great revenues without right.

A man's heart deviseth his way: but the Lord directeth his steps.

Proverbs 16:8,9

A false balance is abomination to the Lord: but a just weight is his delight.

Proverbs 11:1

And thine ears shall hear a word behind thee, saying, This is the way, walk ye in it, when ye turn to the right hand, and when ye turn to the left.

Isaiah 30:21

Thus speaketh the Lord of hosts, saying, Execute true judgment, and shew mercy and compassions every man to his brother.

And oppress not the widow, nor the fatherless, the stranger, nor the poor; and let none of you imagine evil against his brother in your heart.

Zechariah 7:9,10

For with what judgment ye judge, ye shall be judged: and with what measure ye mete, it shall be measured to you again.

Matthew 7:2

Howbeit when he, the Spirit of truth, is come, he will guide you into all truth: for he shall not speak of himself; but whatsoever he shall hear, that shall he speak: and he will shew you things to come.

John 16:13

Then Peter and the other apostles answered and said, We ought to obey God rather than men.

Acts 5:29

For as many as are led by the Spirit of God, they are the sons of God.

Romans 8:14

Being a Father Who Is Faithful

Husbands, love your wives, even as Christ also loved the church, and gave himself for it;

That he might sanctify and cleanse it with the washing of water by the word,

That he might present it to himself a glorious church, not having spot, or wrinkle, or any such thing; but that it should be holy and without blemish.

So ought men to love their wives as their own bodies. He that loveth his wife loveth himself.

For no man ever yet hated his own flesh; but nourisheth and cherisheth it, even as the Lord the church;

For we are members of his body, of his flesh, and of his bones.

For this cause shall a man leave his father and mother, and shall be joined unto his wife, and they two shall be one flesh.

This is a great mystery: but I speak concerning Christ and the church.

Nevertheless let every one of you in particular so love his wife even as himself; and the wife see that she reverence her husband.

Ephesians 5:25-33

My times are in thy hand: deliver me from the hand of mine enemies, and from them that persecute me.

Make thy face to shine upon thy servant: save me for thy mercies' sake.

Psalm 31:15,16

Thou art my hiding place; thou shalt preserve me from trouble; thou shalt compass me about with songs of deliverance.

Psalm 32:7

For the Lord shall be thy confidence.

Proverbs 3:26a

But they that wait upon the Lord shall renew their strength; they shall mount up with wings as eagles; they shall run, and not be weary; and they shall walk, and not faint.

Isaiah 40:31

Therefore all things whatsoever ye would that men should do to you, do ye even so to them: for this is the law and the prophets.

Matthew 7:12

Flee fornication. Every sin that a man doeth is without the body; but he that committeth fornication sinneth against his own body.

1 Corinthians 6:18

And be ye kind one to another, tenderhearted, forgiving one another, even as God for Christ's sake hath forgiven you.

Ephesians 4:32

Being a Father Who Is Kind

Let all bitterness, and wrath, and anger, and clamour, and evil speaking, be put away from you, with all malice.

And be ye kind one to another, tenderhearted, forgiving one another, even as God for Christ's sake hath forgiven you.

Ephesians 4:31,32

Put on therefore, as the elect of God, holy and beloved, bowels of mercies, kindness, humbleness of mind, meekness, longsuffering;

Forbearing one another, and forgiving one another, if any man have a quarrel against any: even as Christ forgave you, so also do ye.

Colossians 3:12,13

Cease from anger, and forsake wrath: fret not thyself in any wise to do evil.

Psalm 37:8

A soft answer turneth away wrath: but grievous words stir up anger.

A wrathful man stirreth up strife: but he that is slow to anger appeaseth strife.

Proverbs 15:1,18

The desire of a man is his kindness; and a poor man is better than a liar.

Proverbs 19:22

He that hath my commandments, and keepeth them, he it is that loveth me: and he that loveth me shall be loved of my Father, and I will love him, and will manifest myself to him.

John 14:21

As the Father hath loved me, so have I loved you: continue ye in my love.

If ye keep my commandments, ye shall abide in my love; even as I have kept my Father's commandments, and abide in his love.

This is my commandment, That ye love one another, as I have loved you.

John 15:9,10,12

But in all things approving ourselves as the ministers of God, in much patience, in afflictions, in necessities, in distresses,

By pureness, by knowledge, by long-suffering, by kindness, by the Holy Ghost, by love unfeigned.

2 Corinthians 6:4,6

And let us not be weary in well doing: for in due season we shall reap, if we faint not.

Galatians 6:9

If You Need Wisdom

Wisdom is the principal thing; therefore get wisdom: and with all thy getting get understanding.

Exalt her, and she shall promote thee: she shall bring thee to honour, when thou dost embrace her.

Proverbs 4:7,8

Through wisdom is an house builded; and by understanding it is established:

And by knowledge shall the chambers be filled with all precious and pleasant riches.

Proverbs 24:3,4

If any of you lack wisdom, let him ask of God, that giveth to all men liberally, and upbraideth not; and it shall be given him.

James 1:5

For the Lord giveth wisdom: out of his mouth cometh knowledge and understanding.

He layeth up sound wisdom for the righteous: he is a buckler to them that walk uprightly.

Proverbs 2:6,7

Trust in the Lord with all thine heart; and lean not unto thine own understanding.

In all thy ways acknowledge him, and he shall direct thy paths.

Proverbs 3:5,6

Whoso loveth instruction loveth knowledge: but he that hateth reproof is brutish.

Proverbs 12:1

He that handleth a matter wisely shall find good: and whoso trusteth in the Lord, happy is he.

The wise in heart shall be called prudent: and the sweetness of the lips increaseth learning.

Understanding is a wellspring of life unto him that hath it: but the instruction of fools is folly.

The heart of the wise teacheth his mouth, and addeth learning to his lips.

Proverbs 16:20-23

My son, be wise, and make my heart glad, that I may answer him that reproacheth me.

Proverbs 27:11

For I will give you a mouth and wisdom, which all your adversaries shall not be able to gainsay nor resist.

Luke 21:15

For to one is given by the Spirit the word of wisdom; to another the word of knowledge by the same Spirit.

1 Corinthians 12:8

If You Have Difficulty Being the Spiritual Leader in Your Home

Only take heed to thyself, and keep thy soul diligently, lest thou forget the things which thine eyes have seen, and lest they depart from thy heart all the days of thy life: but teach them thy sons, and thy sons' sons.

Deuteronomy 4:9

Counsel is mine, and sound wisdom: I am understanding; I have strength.

Proverbs 8:14

Fear thou not; for I am with thee: be not dismayed; for I am thy God: I will strengthen thee; yea, I will help thee; yea, I will uphold thee with the right hand of my righteousness.

Isaiah 41:10

The Lord God is my strength, and he will make my feet like hinds' feet, and he will make me to walk upon mine high places.

Habakkuk 3:19

But ye shall receive power, after that the Holy Ghost is come upon you: and ye shall be witnesses unto me both in Jerusalem, and in all Judaea, and in Samaria, and unto the uttermost part of the earth.

Acts 1:8

Now unto him that is able to do exceeding abundantly above all that we ask or think, according to the power that worketh in us.

Ephesians 3:20

I can do all things through Christ which strengtheneth me.

Philippians 4:13

Strengthened with all might, according to his glorious power, unto all patience and longsuffering with joyfulness.

Colossians 1:11

Cast not away therefore your confidence, which hath great recompense of reward.

For ye have need of patience, that, after ye have done the will of God, ye might receive the promise.

Hebrews 10:35,36

If You Need To Make a Major Career Decision

Trust in the Lord with all thine heart; and lean not unto thine own understanding.

In all thy ways acknowledge him, and he shall direct thy paths.

Proverbs 3:5,6

Thus saith the Lord, thy Redeemer, the Holy One of Israel; I am the Lord thy God which teacheth thee to profit, which leadeth thee by the way that thou shouldest go.

Isaiah 48:17

Howbeit when he, the Spirit of truth, is come, he will guide you into all truth: for he shall not speak of himself; but whatsoever he shall hear, that shall he speak: and he will shew you things to come.

He shall glorify me: for he shall receive of mine, and shall shew it unto you.

John 16:13,14

If any of you lack wisdom, let him ask of God that giveth to all men liberally, and upbraideth not; and it shall be given him.

James 1:5

And the Lord, he it is that doth go before thee; he will be with thee, he will not fail thee, neither forsake thee: fear not, neither be dismayed.

Deuteronomy 31:8

Have not I commanded thee? Be strong and of a good courage, be not afraid, neither be thou dismayed: for the Lord thy God is with thee whithersoever thou goest.

Joshua 1:9

Be ye strong therefore, and let not your hands be weak: for your work shall be rewarded.

2 Chronicles 15:7

I will bless the lord, who hath given me counsel: my reins also instruct me in the night seasons.

Psalm 16:7

Shew me thy ways, O Lord; teach me thy paths.

Psalm 25:4

I will instruct thee and teach thee in the way which thou shalt go: I will guide thee with mine eye.

Psalm 32:8

If You Need Peace Within

Peace I leave with you, my peace I give unto you: not as the world giveth, give I unto you. Let not your heart be troubled, neither let it be afraid.

John 14:27

Be careful for nothing; but in every thing by prayer and supplication with thanksgiving let your requests be made known unto God.

And the peace of God, which passeth all understanding, shall keep your hearts and minds through Christ Jesus.

Those things, which ye have both learned, and received, and heard, and seen in me, do: and the God of peace shall be with you.

Philippians 4:6,7,9

And let the peace of God rule in your hearts, to the which also ye are called in one body; and be ye thankful.

Colossians 3:15

I will both lay me down in peace, and sleep: for thou, Lord, only makest me dwell in safety.

Psalm 4:8

What man is he that feareth the Lord? him shall he teach in the way that he shall choose.

His soul shall dwell at ease; and his seed shall inherit the earth.

Psalm 25:12,13

Thou wilt keep him in perfect peace, whose mind is stayed on thee: because he trusteth in thee.

Lord, thou wilt ordain peace for us: for thou also hast wrought all our works in us.

Isaiah 26:3,12

For ye shall go out with joy, and be led forth with peace: the mountains and the hills shall break forth before you into singing, and all the trees of the field shall clap their hands.

Isaiah 55:12

He shall enter into peace: they shall rest in their beds, each one walking in his uprightness.

Isaiah 57:2

These things I have spoken unto you, that in me ye might have peace. In the world ye shall have tribulation: but be of good cheer; I have overcome the world.

John 16:33

Therefore being justified by faith, we have peace with God through our Lord Jesus Christ.

Romans 5:1

If You Need To Forgive

And when ye stand praying, forgive, if ye have ought against any: that your Father also which is in heaven may forgive you your trespasses.

Mark 11:25

Take heed to yourselves: If thy brother trespass against thee, rebuke him; and if he repent, forgive him.

And if he trespasses against thee seven times in a day, and seven times in a day turn again to thee, saying, I repent; thou shalt forgive him.

Luke 17:3,4

And be ye kind one to another, tenderhearted, forgiving one another, even as God for Christ's sake hath forgiven you.

Ephesians 4:32

But I say unto you, Love your enemies, bless them that curse you, do good to them that hate you, and pray for them which despitefully use you, and persecute you.

Matthew 5:44

And forgive us our debts, as we forgive our debtors.

For if ye forgive men their trespasses, your heavenly Father will also forgive you.

But if ye forgive not men their trespasses, neither will your Father forgive your trespasses.

Matthew 6:12,14,15

Then came Peter to him, and said, Lord, how oft shall my brother sin against me, and I forgive him? till seven times?

Jesus saith unto him, I say not unto thee, Until seven times: but, Until seventy times seven.

Matthew 18:21,22

Whose soever sins ye remit, they are remitted unto them; and whose soever sins ye retain, they are retained.

John 20:23

Bless them which persecute you: bless, and curse not.

Be not overcome of evil, but overcome evil with good.

Romans 12:14,21

Forbearing one another, and forgiving one another, if any man have a quarrel against any: even as Christ forgave you, so also do ye.

Colossians 3:13

If You Need To Overcome Anger

Now the works of the flesh are manifest, which are these; Adultery, fornication, uncleanness, lasciviousness.

Idolatry, witchcraft, hatred, variance, emulations, wrath, strife, seditions, heresies.

Envyings, murders, drunkenness, revellings, and such like: of the which I tell you before, as I have also told you in time past, that they which do such things shall not inherit the kingdom of God.

But the fruit of the Spirit is love, joy, peace, longsuffering, gentleness, goodness, faith.

Meekness, temperance: against such there is no law.

And they that are Christ's have crucified the flesh with the affections and lusts.

If we live in the Spirit, let us also walk in the Spirit.

Let us not be desirous of vain glory, provoking one another, envying one another.

Galatians 5:19-26

Be ye angry, and sin not: let not the sun go down upon your wrath.

Let all bitterness, and wrath, and anger, and clamour, and evil speaking, be put away from you, with all malice.

And be ye kind one to another, tenderhearted, forgiving one another, even as God for Christ's sake hath forgiven you.

Ephesians 4:26,31,32

Be not hasty in thy spirit to be angry: for anger resteth in the bosom of fools.

Ecclesiastes 7:9

The Lord God hath given me the tongue of the learned, that I should know how to speak a word in season to him that is weary: he wakeneth morning by morning, he wakeneth mine ear to hear as the learned.

Isaiah 50:4

Blessed are the peacemakers: for they shall be called the children of God.

Matthew 5:9

For to be carnally minded is death; but to be spiritually minded is life and peace.

Romans 8:6

Let nothing be done through strife or vainglory; but in lowliness of mind let each esteem other better than themselves.

Look not every man on his own things, but every man also on the things of others.

Philippians 2:3,4

If You Need Motivation

Be strong and of a good courage, fear not, nor be afraid of them: for the Lord thy God, he it is that doth go with thee; he will not fail thee, nor forsake thee.

Deuteronomy 31:6

Verily, verily, I say unto you, He that believeth on me, the works that I do shall he do also; and greater works than these shall he do; because I go unto my Father.

John 14:12

I can do all things through Christ which strengtheneth me.

Philippians 4:13

Beloved, I wish above all things that thou mayest prosper and be in health, even as thy soul prospereth.

3 John 2

There shall no man be able to stand before you: for the Lord your God shall lay the fear of you and the dread of you upon all the land that ye shall tread upon, as he hath said unto you.

Deuteronomy 11:25

The Lord shall cause thine enemies that rise up against thee to be smitten before thy face: they shall come out against thee one way, and flee before thee seven ways.

Deuteronomy 28:7

Be strong and of a good courage: for unto this people shalt thou divide for an inheritance the land, which I sware unto their fathers to give them.

Joshua 1:6

For the lord hath driven out from before you great nations and strong: but as for you, no man hath been able to stand before you unto this day.

Joshua 23:9

David encouraged himself in the Lord his God.

1 Samuel 30:6b

And he answered, Fear not: for they that be with us are more than they that be with them.

2 Kings 6:16

The Spirit of the Lord God is upon me; because the Lord hath anointed me to preach good tidings unto the meek; he hath sent me to bind up the brokenhearted, to proclaim liberty to the captives, and the opening of the prison to them that are bound.

Isaiah 61:1

If Your Job Is Unsatisfying

I will instruct thee and teach thee in the way which thou shalt go: I will guide thee with mine eye.

Psalm 32:8

Therefore, my beloved brethren, be ye stedfast, unmoveable, always abounding in the work of the Lord, forasmuch as ye know that your labour is not in vain in the Lord.

1 Corinthians 15:58

And that ye study to be quiet, and to do your own business, and to work with your own hands, as we commanded you;

That ye may walk honestly toward them that are without, and that ye may have lack of nothing.

1 Thessalonians 4:11,12

Be of good courage, and he shall strengthen your heart, all ye that hope in the Lord.

Psalm 31:24

For in thee, O Lord, do I hope: thou wilt hear, O Lord my God.

Psalm 38:15

Why art thou cast down, O my soul? and why art thou disquieted within me? hope in God: for I shall yet praise him, who is the health of my countenance, and my God.

Psalm 43:5

But I will hope continually, and will yet praise thee more and more.

Psalm 71:14

Happy is he that hath the God of Jacob for his help, whose hope is in the Lord his God.

Psalm 146:5

Keep thy heart with all diligence; for out of it are the issues of life.

Proverbs 4:23

The hand of the diligent shall bear rule: but the slothful shall be under tribute.

Proverbs 12:24

Hope deferred maketh the heart sick: but when the desire cometh, it is a tree of life.

Proverbs 13:12

Love not sleep, lest thou come to poverty; open thine eyes, and thou shalt be satisfied with bread.

Proverbs 20:13

Let not thine heart envy sinners: but be thou in the fear of the Lord all the day long.

For surely there is an end; and thine expectations shall not be cut off.

Proverbs 23:17,18

If You Feel Like a Failure

He that dwelleth in the secret place of the most High shall abide under the shadow of the Almighty.

I will say of the Lord, He is my refuge and my fortress: my God; in him will I trust.

Psalm 91:1,2

Thou wilt keep him in perfect peace, whose mind is stayed on thee: because he trusteth in thee.

Isaiah 26:3

If we confess our sins, he is faithful and just to forgive us our sins, and to cleanse us from all unrighteousness.

1 John 1:9

But he knoweth the way that I take: when he hath tried me, I shall come forth as gold.

Job 23:10

He will keep the feet of his saints, and the wicked shall be silent in darkness; for by strength shall no man prevail.

1 Samuel 2:9

I will both lay me down in peace, and sleep: for thou, Lord, only makest me dwell in safety.

Psalm 4:8

As far as the east is from the west, so far hath he removed our transgressions from us.

Psalm 103:12

When thou liest down, thou shalt not be afraid: yea, thou shalt lie down, and thy sleep shall be sweet.

Proverbs 3:24

I, even I, am he that blotteth out thy transgressions for mine own sake, and will not remember thy sins.

Isaiah 43:25

Let the wicked forsake his way, and the unrighteous man his thoughts; and let him return unto the Lord, and he will have mercy upon him; and to our God, for he will abundantly pardon.

Isaiah 55:7

The Lord thy God in the midst of thee is mighty; he will save, he will rejoice over thee with joy; he will rest in his love, he will joy over thee with singing.

Zephaniah 3:17

For he hath made him to be sin for us, who knew no sin; that we might be made the righteousness of God in him.

2 Corinthians 5:21

If You Are Facing Sexual Temptation

Watch and pray, that ye enter not into temptation: the spirit indeed is willing, but the flesh is weak.

Matthew 26:41

There hath no temptation taken you but such as is common to man: but God is faithful, who will not suffer you to be tempted above that ye are able; but will with the temptation also make a way to escape, that ye may be able to bear it.

1 Corinthians 10:13

Let no man say when he is tempted, I am tempted of God: for God cannot be tempted with evil, neither tempteth he any man:

But every man is tempted, when he is drawn away of his own lust, and enticed.

James 1:13,14

The Lord knoweth how to deliver the godly out of temptations, and to reserve the unjust unto the day of judgment to be punished.

2 Peter 2:9

But thou, O Lord, art a shield for me; my glory, and the lifter up of mine head.

Psalm 3:3

Let integrity and uprightness preserve me; for I wait on thee.

Psalm 25:21

Judge me, O Lord; for I have walked in mine integrity: I have trusted also in the Lord; therefore I shall not slide.

But as for me, I will walk in mine integrity: redeem me, and be merciful unto me.

Psalm 26:1,11

Be pleased, O Lord, to deliver me: O Lord, make haste to help me.

Let them be ashamed and confounded together that seek after my soul to destroy it; let them be driven backward and put to shame that wish me evil.

Psalm 40:13,14

It is better to trust in the Lord than to put confidence in man.

Psalm 118:8

Thy word have I hid in mine heart, that I might not sin against thee.

Psalm 119:11

For the Lord shall be thy confidence, and shall keep thy foot from being taken.

Proverbs 3:26

If Your Wife Is Unsupportive of Your Dreams and Goals

The Lord is my light and my salvation; whom shall I fear? the Lord is the strength of my life; of whom shall I be afraid?

Thou an host should encamp against me, my heart shall not fear: though war should rise against me, in this will I be confident.

Wait on the Lord: be of good courage, and he shall strengthen thine heart: wait, I say, on the Lord.

Psalm 27:1,3,14

For thou art my rock and my fortress; therefore for thy name's sake lead me, and guide me.

Pull me out of the net that they have laid privily for me: for thou art my strength.

Psalm 31:3,4

Thou art my hiding place; thou shalt preserve me from trouble; thou shalt compass me about with songs of deliverance.

I will instruct thee and teach thee in the way which thou shalt go: I will guide thee with mine eye.

Psalm 32:7,8

My soul melteth for heaviness: strengthen thou me according unto thy word.

Psalm 119:28

Hatred stirreth up strifes: but love covereth all sins.

Proverbs 10:12

A friend loveth at all times, and a brother is born for adversity.

Proverbs 17:17

A new commandment I give unto you, That ye love one another; as I have loved you, that ye also love one another.

John 13:34

I know both how to be abased, and I know how to abound: every where and in all things I am instructed both to be full and to be hungry, both to abound and to suffer need.

I can do all things through Christ which strengtheneth me.

But my God shall supply all your need according to his riches in glory by Christ Jesus.

Philippians 4:12,13,19

Forbearing one another, and forgiving one another, if any man have a quarrel against any: even as Christ forgave you, so also do ye.

And above all these things put on charity, which is the bond of perfectness.

Colossians 3:13,14

If Your Wife Has Responsibilities out of the Home

Can two walk together, except they be agreed?

Amos 3:3

I will bless the Lord, who hath given me counsel: my reins also instruct me in the night seasons.

Psalm 16:7

As for God, his way is perfect: the word of the Lord is tried: he is a buckler to all those that trust in him.

Psalm 18:30

Great peace have they which love thy law: and nothing shall offend them.

Psalm 119:165

The Lord will perfect that which concerneth me: thy mercy, O Lord, endureth for ever: forsake not the works of thine own hands.

Psalm 138:8

Counsel is mine, and sound wisdom: I am understanding; I have strength.

Proverbs 8:14

Trust in the Lord with all thine heart; and lean not unto thine own understanding.

In all thy ways acknowledge him, and he shall direct thy paths.

Proverbs 3:5,6

Understanding is a wellspring of life unto him that hath it: but the instruction of fools is folly.

The heart of the wise teacheth his mouth, and addeth learning to his lips.

Proverbs 16:22,23

Through wisdom is an house builded; and by understanding it is established:

And by knowledge shall the chambers be filled with all precious and pleasant riches.

Proverbs 24:3,4

Behold, God is my salvation; I will trust, and not be afraid: for the Lord Jehovah is my strength and my song; he also is become my salvation.

Isaiah 12:2

For my thoughts are not your thoughts, neither are your ways my ways, saith the Lord.

For as the heavens are higher than the earth, so are my ways higher than your ways, and my thoughts than your thoughts.

Isaiah 55:8,9

Call unto me, and I will answer thee, and shew thee great and mighty things, which thou knowest not.

Jeremiah 33:3

If Your Daily Family Devotions Seem Difficult

Train up a child in the way he should go: and when he is old, he will not depart from it.

Proverbs 22:6

And all thy children shall be taught of the Lord; and great shall be the peace of thy children.

In righteousness shalt thou be established: thou shalt be far from oppression; for thou shalt not fear: and from terror; for it shall not come near thee.

Isaiah 54:13,14

But if any provide not for his own, and specially for those of his own house, he hath denied the faith, and is worse than an infidel.

1 Timothy 5:8

A good man leaveth an inheritance to his children's children: and the wealth of the sinner is laid up for the just.

Proverbs 13:22

The just man walketh in his integrity: his children are blessed after him.

Proverbs 20:7

The father of the righteous shall greatly rejoice: and he that begetteth a wise child shall have joy of him.

Proverbs 23:24

Through wisdom is an house builded; and by understanding it is established.

Proverbs 24:3

Correct thy son, and he shall give thee rest; yea, he shall give delight unto thy soul.

Proverbs 29:17

Tell ye your children of it, and let your children tell their children, and their children another generation.

Joel 1:3

But seek ye first the kingdom of God, and his righteousness; and all these things shall be added unto you.

Matthew 6:33

And, ye fathers, provoke not your children to wrath: but bring them up in the nurture and admonition of the Lord.

Ephesians 6:4

If Your Child Is Rebellious Toward You

Now therefore go, and I will be with thy mouth, and teach thee what thou shalt say.

Exodus 4:12

Behold, to obey is better than sacrifice, and to hearken than the fat of rams.

For rebellion is as the sin of witchcraft, and stubbornness is as iniquity and idolatry. Because thou hast rejected the word of the Lord, he hath also rejected thee from being king.

1 Samuel 15:22b,23

Teach me, and I will hold my tongue: and cause me to understand wherein I have erred.

Job 6:24

Shew me thy ways, O Lord; teach me thy paths.

What man is he that feareth the Lord? him shall he teach in the way that he shall choose.

Psalm 25:4,12

I had fainted, unless I had believed to see the goodness of the Lord in the land of the living.

Wait on the Lord: be of good courage, and he shall strengthen thine heart: wait, I say, on the Lord.

Psalm 27:13,14

The Lord is my strength and my shield; my heart trusted in him, and I am helped: therefore my heart greatly rejoiceth; and with my song will I praise him.

Psalm 28:7

Cast thy burden upon the Lord, and he shall sustain thee: he shall never suffer the righteous to be moved.

Psalm 55:22

Though I walk in the midst of trouble, thou wilt revive me: thou shalt stretch forth thine hand against the wrath of mine enemies, and thy right hand shall save me.

Psalm 138:7

Teach me to do thy will; for thou art my God: thy spirit is good; lead me into the land of uprightness.

Psalm 143:10

Keep my commandments, and live; and my law as the apple of thine eye.

Proverbs 7:2

If Your Child Is Rebellious Toward God

And he shall turn the heart of the fathers to the children, and the heart of the children to their fathers, lest I come and smite the earth with a curse.

Malachi 4:6

And, ye fathers, provoke not your children to wrath: but bring them up in the nurture and admonition of the Lord.

Ephesians 6:4

Now faith is the substance of things hoped for, the evidence of things not seen.

But without faith it is impossible to please him: for he that cometh to God must believe that he is, and that he is a rewarder of them that diligently seek him.

Hebrews 11:1,6

Wait on the Lord: be of good courage, and he shall strengthen thine heart: wait, I say, on the Lord.

Psalm 27:14

Our soul waiteth for the Lord: he is our help and our shield.

Psalm 33:20

Delight thyself also in the Lord; and he shall give thee the desires of thine heart.

Commit thy way unto the Lord; trust also in him; and he shall bring it to pass.

Psalm 37:4,5

Cast thy burden upon the Lord, and he shall sustain thee: he shall never suffer the righteous to be moved.

Psalm 55:22

For the Lord will not cast off his people, neither will he forsake his inheritance.

Psalm 94:14

I wait for the Lord, my soul doth wait, and in his word do I hope.

Psalm 130:5

The Lord will perfect that which concerneth me: thy mercy, O Lord, endureth for ever: forsake not the works of thine own hands.

Psalm 138:8

Children's children are the crown of old men; and the glory of children are their fathers.

Proverbs 17:6

Correct thy son, and he shall give thee rest; yea, he shall give delight unto thy soul.

Proverbs 29:17

If Your Child Is Withdrawing From You

I sought the Lord, and he heard me, and delivered me from all my fears.

Psalm 34:4

Be still, and know that I am God.

Psalm 46:10

He will not suffer thy foot to be moved: he that keepeth thee will not slumber.

Psalm 121:3

For I was an hungred, and ye gave me meat: I was thirsty, and ye gave me drink: I was a stranger, and ye took me in.

Naked, and ye clothed me: I was sick, and ye visited me: I was in prison, and ye came unto me.

Then shall the righteous answer him, saying, Lord, when saw we thee an hungred, and fed thee? or thirsty, and gave thee drink?

When saw we thee a stranger, and took thee in? or naked, and clothed thee? Or when saw we thee sick, or in prison, and came unto thee?

And the King shall answer and say unto them, Verily I say unto you, Inasmuch as ye have done it unto one of the least of these my brethren, ye have done it unto me.

Matthew 25:35-40

In your patience possess ye your souls.

Luke 21:19

I will not leave you comfortless: I will come to you.

John 14:18

And not only so, but we glory in tribulations also: knowing that tribulation worketh patience.

And patience, experience; and experience, hope.

And hope maketh not ashamed; because the love of God is shed abroad in our hearts by the Holy Ghost which is given unto us.

Romans 5:3-5

Bear ye one another's burdens, and so fulfill the law of Christ.

Galatians 6:2

For God is not unrighteous to forget your work and labour of love, which ye have shewed toward his name, in that ye have ministered to the saints, and do minister.

Hebrews 6:10

If Your Child Encounters Peer Pressure

The Lord also will be a refuge for the oppressed, a refuge in times of trouble.

Psalm 9:9

I will love thee, O Lord, my strength.

The Lord is my rock, and my fortress, and my deliverer; my God, my strength, in whom I will trust; my buckler, and the horn of my salvation, and my high tower.

Psalm 18:1,2

My flesh and my heart faileth: but God is the strength of my heart, and my portion for ever.

Psalm 73:26

A thousand shall fall at thy side, and ten thousand at thy right hand; but it shall not come nigh thee.

There shall no evil befall thee, neither shall any plague come nigh thy dwelling.

Psalm 91:7,10

Bless the Lord, O my soul, and forget not all his benefits.

Who satisfieth thy mouth with good things; so that thy youth is renewed like the eagle's.

Psalm 103:2,5

He sent his word, and healed them, and delivered them from their destructions.

Psalm 107:20

Peace be within thy walls, and prosperity within thy palaces.

Psalm 122:7

It is vain for you to rise up early, to sit up late, to eat the bread of sorrows: for so he giveth his beloved sleep.

Psalm 127:2

When thou liest down, thou shalt not be afraid: yea, thou shalt lie down, and thy sleep shall be sweet.

Proverbs 3:24

The wicked are overthrown, and are not: but the house of the righteous shall stand.

Proverbs 12:7

But they that wait upon the Lord shall renew their strength; they shall mount up with wings as eagles; they shall run, and not be weary; and they shall walk, and not faint.

Isaiah 40:31

If Your Child Has a Poor Self-Image

And God said, Let us make man in our image, after our likeness: and let them have dominion over the fish of the sea, and over the fowl of the air, and over the cattle, and over all the earth, and over every creeping thing that creepeth upon the earth.

So God created man in his own image, in the image of God created he him; male and female created he them.

Genesis 1:26,27

Of the Rock that begat thee thou art unmindful, and hast forgotten God that formed thee.

Deuteronomy 32:18

David said moreover, The Lord that delivered me out of the paw of the lion, and out of the paw of the bear, he will deliver me out of the hand of this Philistine. And Saul said unto David, Go, and the Lord be with thee.

1 Samuel 17:37

But thou, O Lord, are a shield for me; my glory, and the lifter up of mine head.

Psalm 3:3

I will not be afraid of ten thousands of people, that have set themselves against me round about.

Psalm 3:6

The Lord is my light and my salvation; whom shall I fear? the Lord is the strength of my life; of whom shall I be afraid?

Though an host should encamp against me, my heart shall not fear: though war should rise against me, in this will I be confident.

For in the time of trouble he shall hide me in his pavilion: in the secret of his tabernacle shall he hide me; he shall set me up upon a rock.

Psalm 27:1,3,5

It is better to trust in the Lord than to put confidence in man.

Psalm 118:8

Thy word have I hid in mine heart, that I might not sin against thee.

Psalm 119:11

For the Lord shall be thy confidence, and shall keep thy foot from being taken.

Proverbs 3:26

In the fear of the Lord is strong confidence: and his children shall have a place of refuge.

Proverbs 14:26

If Your Child Is Sick

Bless the Lord, O my soul, and forget not all his benefits.

Who forgiveth all thine iniquities; who healeth all thy diseases.

Psalm 103:2,3

Surely he hath borne our griefs, and carried our sorrows: yet we did esteem him stricken, smitten of God, and afflicted. But he was wounded for our transgressions, he was bruised for our iniquities: the chastisement of our peace was upon him; and with his stripes we are healed.

Isaiah 53:4,5

Is any among you afflicted? let him pray. Is any merry? let him sing psalms.

Is any sick among you? let him call for the elders of the church; and let them pray over him, anointing him with oil in the name of the Lord.

And the prayer of faith shall save the sick, and the Lord shall raise him up; and if he have committed sins, they shall be forgiven him.

Confess your faults one to another, and pray one for another, that ye may be healed. The effectual fervent prayer of a righteous man availeth much.

James 5:13-16

Beloved, I wish above all things that thou mayest prosper and be in health, even as thy soul prospereth.

3 John 2

And the Lord will take away from thee all sickness, and will put none of the evil diseases of Egypt, which thou knowest, upon thee; but will lay them upon all them that hate thee.

Deuteronomy 7:15

My son, attend to my words; incline thine ear unto my sayings.

Let them not depart from thine eyes; keep them in the midst of thine heart.

For they are life unto those that find them, and health to all their flesh.

Proverbs 4:20-22

Heal me, O Lord, and I shall be healed; save me, and I shall be saved: for thou art my praise.

Jeremiah 17:14

For I will restore health unto thee, and I will heal thee of thy wounds, saith the Lord.

Jeremiah 30:17a

Part III
The Family Man

The Making of a Family
by Richard Exley

The family is not a cultural phenomenon to be discarded with the changing times. It was conceived in the mind of God. It is the loving gift of a wise and generous Creator. Knowing the unique needs of the man created in His own image, God said: ". . . 'It is not good for the man to be alone. I will make a helper suitable for him'" (Gen. 2:18).

> ". . . So the LORD God caused the man to fall into a deep sleep and while he was sleeping, he took one of the man's ribs and closed up the place with flesh. Then the LORD God made a woman from the rib he had taken out of the man, and he brought her to the man."
>
> **Genesis 2:21,22**

Now the man is no longer alone. He has a companion, someone to love and someone to love him, and a helper. Think of that — God made them helpers, one for the other. And He blessed that union and called it "family." Therefore, we must conclude that God intended for the family to be a helping place. And when it functions as God intended, that's what it is. It provides a loving community in which a child is "helped" to develop his gifts and potentials. It is a safe place in which a child is "helped" to develop the people skills so necessary to live meaningfully in our complex society. And it is a sanctuary in which he is "helped" to learn spiritual values and develop a personal relationship with the living God.

Obviously the most important thing in creating a family is time — time to be together, time to love one another, time to share life's experiences, both great and small.

Unfortunately, time seems to be the thing we find hardest to give.

In *What Wives Wish Their Husbands Knew About Women*, Dr. Dobson quotes from an article by Dr. Branfenbrenner, in which he decries the plague of parental absence: "The demands of a job that claim meal times, evenings and weekends as well as day; the trips and moves necessary to get ahead or simply to hold one's own; the increasing time spent communicating, entertaining, going out, meeting social and community obligations, all these produce a situation in which a child often spends more time with a passive babysitter than with a participating parent."[1]

Dr. Dobson then proceeds to substantiate Branfenbrenner's observations: "A team of researchers wanted to learn how much time middle-class fathers spend playing and interacting with their small children. First, they asked a group of fathers to estimate the time spent with their one-year-old youngsters each day, and received an average reply of fifteen to twenty minutes. To verify these claims, the investigators attached microphones to the shirts of small children for the purpose of recording actual parental verbalization. The results are shocking: *The average amount of time spent by these middle-class fathers with their small children was thirty-seven seconds per day!* Their direct interaction was limited to 2.7 encounters daily lasting ten to fifteen seconds each."[2] (emphasis mine)

It goes almost without saying that the children of such fathers will grow up lacking the sense of family which is absolutely vital to a healthy self-image. Depending upon their motivation, their skills, and their intellect, they may go on to become outstanding successes in their chosen fields. But without a special healing they will not be fulfilled; they will not escape the nagging questions they have about their value as persons. Still, the greatest tragedy may be the fact that they will "sin" against their children in the same way their parents "sinned" against them, thus perpetuating this tragedy from generation to generation. And the likelihood of this happening increases, almost daily, as our world becomes more and more impersonal.

In order to break this deadly cycle, the person driven by self-doubts must find emotional healing in the presence of God, and through the dynamic fellowship of committed believers. He must find a surrogate family, a place to belong. As unlikely as this may sound to the person who has been "alone" all his life, it is possible. In fact, it is happening with increasing frequency. As the Church learns more and more about the relationship between community and personal wholeness, it is providing greater ministry in this area. Over and over again, through the years, I have witnessed God's healing love manifested through small groups of loving believers. The miracles are seldom instantaneous, but they are, nonetheless, dramatic. Take the case of Sterling, for instance:

"I first met him when he came to my office for pastoral counseling. He was only a few days removed from the county jail and newly converted. . . .

"He never knew his father, and his mother abandoned him when he was just a small boy. A kindly aunt took him in and reared him as her own. Still, her love could not heal the wound his parents' rejection has inflicted. By the time he was fourteen, he was a confirmed alcoholic and constantly in trouble with the authorities.

"His incorrigible behavior finally resulted in his being sent to reform school. Unfortunately, that intensified his anger and bitterness, and upon his release he immediately returned to his antisocial behavior. Soon he was serving a sentence in the state penitentiary, then another.

"When he came to see me, he was out on bail awaiting trial for allegedly raping his sixteen-year-old stepdaughter.

While in the county jail, he had started reading the Bible and was born again. Now he wanted to know if he could become part of our church. I assured him that he could, and soon he was deeply involved in the life of our fellowship including a growth group which I led once a week. I can still remember the night he told us that he finally felt loved, for the first time in his life, by God and by the group."[3]

At last he was free from his parents' rejection and the debilitating wounds it had left. Now he could get on with the business of becoming a loving husband and father in his own right. It wouldn't be easy, because he had a lifetime of negative behavior to "unlearn," but he knew that with God's help and the support of the group it was possible.

I share Sterling's story, extreme though it is, to make a point. If God could do that for him, then surely He can heal the fears and insecurities that haunt you. There is hope for your family!

And, even if you grew up in a family rich with love and acceptance, you will still need God's help to be the kind of parent your children need. Given the pressures we all face, only a determined decision, backed up by divine help, will enable us to give our families the spiritual and emotional support they must have. As I look back over the past 22 years of marriage, I can testify to God's sufficiency and His faithfulness.

Until Leah entered the fifth grade, her mother and I were serving pastorates in small churches in remote rural areas. Financially, it was a hardship, but what we lacked in money was more than made up for in family time. My office was in the house, so I was always near Leah. Some of my best memories are of her interrupting my sermon preparation for a little tender loving care. Until she was in the sixth grade I was able to drive her to school every morning and pick her up every afternoon. Those were our special times. I'll never forget how she looked bounding down the hill toward the car, her fists full of papers, her hair backlighted by the afternoon sun.

Inspired by the example left us by our parents, Brenda and I determined to continue the holy heritage of family. In the winter we all went snowmobiling in the countryside and ice skating in the park. In the summer we hiked and picnicked in the mountains. In the fall we cut firewood, buoyed by the prospect of long winter evenings together in front of a roaring fire. We became "photography nuts," and we now have hundreds of pictures, and even more memories.

I will always be thankful I was free to be a father when Leah needed me most. Still, it was a choice. There were many things I could have done, but I chose to spend my time and energy being a husband and a father. What are you choosing?

In addition to time, children must have unconditional parental love if they are to grow up to be emotionally whole adults. In my work with professional groups, I frequently encounter men and women who overreact to the smallest slight, real or imagined. Others are defensive, while still others are withdrawn or have trouble relating to persons in authority. Again and again these difficulties have their roots in the parent-child relationship. As a general rule such people did not receive their parents' unconditional love when they were children. As a consequence, they are not emotionally whole persons.

Unconditional love is not dependent upon the child's performance. It is given freely, consistently. It enables a child to unconsciously separate his value as a person from his performance, good or bad. Unconditional love can be expressed in a variety of ways, but none is more effective than touching and telling. All children need to be held and hugged. They need to hear their parents say the three most powerful words in the human vocabulary — "I love you."

Almost four years ago, I was on my way to Anchorage, Alaska, and I finally had a few hours to myself. There were no phones to answer, no deadlines to meet, and no one scheduled for counseling. After a couple of hours I began to wind down, and as I did, I grew nostalgic, or philosophical, maybe both. Not being one to waste such feelings, I wrote my daughter a letter. I would like to share some of it with you:

"Dear Leah,

"It's been a while since I've told you what a special person you are. God has given you the gift of joy and self-confidence. I think you have tremendous people skills, and a real talent for public speaking and drama. When I was your age I was shy and introverted; my gifts were not developed at all. You are years ahead of me and I believe your accomplishments will far exceed my own. Never forget, though, that when God gives a person special gifts, He also gives them special responsibilities.

"I hope I've rubbed off on you these past fifteen years. I want you to catch the values which make my life rich. Here's a partial list of the things I hope you remember when you are grown and on your own.

"1. Attitude is everything — it can make or break you. It is the one thing no one can ever take from you — the freedom to choose how you are going to feel about a given situation. As the poet put it, 'Two men looked out through the prison bars; one man saw the mud, one man saw the stars.'

"2. Relationships are the most important things in life. Do unto others as you would have them do unto you. Always be careful to use things and love people.

"3. Don't be afraid to fail. Nothing great was ever achieved on the first try. Learn from your failures and try again.

"4. God's will is not inhibiting. It frees you to fulfill your highest potential, while enjoying the most meaningful life possible.

"5. If you sin, God always stands ready to forgive. In fact, He is always more anxious to forgive us than we are to be forgiven.

"6. True joy is found in striving for God-given goals, even more than in obtaining them; so dare to dream big dreams, dare to attempt great things for God.

"That's enough for today. Let me close with some things I hope you remember when you are grown and gone. I hope you remember how crazy funny I can be when it's just the three of us and I'm letting my hair down. I hope you remember how much I love your mother and how special I think she is. I hope you remember how conscientious I was, how hard I worked, and how deeply I cared for people. Most of all I want you to remember how much I love God and how special you are to me. Never forget that I love you unconditionally. There is nothing you can do, no success or achievement, which will ever make me love you more. I love you, not because of what you do, but because of who you are.

"With all my love,

"Dad"

Boys need that kind of affirming love, too. Betsy Lee, in *Miracle in the Making*, writes: "My mother grew up in a family of girls. She was comfortable raising my sister and me, but my brother John confounded her from the day he was born.

"Distance loomed between Mom and John. She wasn't sure how to express her affection or tame his wild spirit. She seemed constantly to warn him of dangers.

"John frequently whined, 'You're always telling me that.'

"Mother always explained that her instructions were for his benefit. 'What do you think a mother is for?' she added.

"'To love me,' he said.

"My mother was stunned, but prudent enough not to be defensive. She sought to change the way she communicated her love.

"My aunt, who had raised a son, told my mother, 'Boys aren't any different from girls. They need to be touched and kissed goodnight.' This came as a revelation to my mother, who thought cuddling would compromise her son's masculinity. But as soon as she started to demonstrate her love in direct, visible ways, John responded with greater warmth, and he began to respect her authority.

"As in all relationships, love had to be expressed in words and actions in order to grow."[4]

Some parents get the wrong impression when we talk of loving our children unconditionally. They mistakenly think that means they should never discipline their offspring. Nothing could be further from the truth. In fact, without proper discipline children will be unsure of their parents' love. When used appropriately, discipline is an act of love; it also creates a feeling of security by clearly defining the boundaries of behavior.

Discipline without love is tyrannical; it produces dependent people who are both hostile and fearful. Love without discipline is permissive; it trains children to be selfish and obnoxious. But when unconditional love and consistent discipline are both present in the family structure, they produce children who are emotionally healthy and well-adjusted.

"Dr. Stanley Coopersmith, associate professor of psychology, University of California, studied 1,738 normal middle-class boys and their families, beginning in the pre-adolescent period and following them through to young manhood. After identifying those boys having the highest self-esteem, he compared their homes and childhood influences with those having a lower sense of self-worth. He found three important characteristics which distinguished them:

"1. The high-esteem children clearly were more loved and appreciated at home than were the low-esteem boys.

"2. The high-esteem group came from homes where parents had been significantly more strict in their approach to discipline. By contrast, the parents of the low-esteem group had created insecurity and dependence by their permissiveness.

"3. The homes of the high-esteem group were also characterized by democracy and openness. Once the boundaries for behavior were established, there was freedom for individual personalities to grow and develop. The boys could express themselves without fear of ridicule, and the overall atmosphere was marked by acceptance and emotional safety."[5]

To fully satisfy the growing child's spiritual and emotional needs, the family must also provide spiritual training. While this should definitely include some form of graduated family devotions, designed with the child's needs in mind, in truth the most effective training grows out of real-life experiences. The most productive parents are those who watch for these special moments and make the most of them.

It has been called "striking while the iron is hot," a phrase which comes out of the old village blacksmith's shop. It refers to that precise moment when the metal has been heated to the exact temperature at which it is the most malleable. Life, too, has a way of creating situations like that in the experience of every child. Moments when circumstances have sensitized him to spiritual truths. The perceptive parent seizes those opportunities and, as a result, life-transforming truth is planted deep in the child's soul.

Take the time to allow your family to develop as God intended. Take the time to help your children develop their gifts and potentials, their people skills. Take the time to help them learn spiritual values and to form a deep personal relationship with the living God. And take the time to be together, to love one another, to share life's experiences both great and small.

Endnotes

[1] James Dobson, *What Wives Wish Their Husbands Knew About Women* (Wheaton: Tyndale House Publishers, Inc., 1975), p. 158.

[2] Ibid.

[3] Richard Exley, *Blue-Collar Christianity* (Tulsa: Honor Books, 1989), pp. 193,194.

[4] Reprinted by permission from *Miracle in the Making* by Betsy Lee, copyright © 1983, Augsburg Publishing House.

[5] James Dobson, *Hide and Seek, Self-Esteem for the Child* (Old Tappan: Fleming H. Revell, 1979), pp. 92,93.

[6] William Barclay, *The New Testament: A New Translation, Volume Two, The Letters and the Revelation* (London: Collins Publishers, 1969), p. 120.

Part IV
Getting Into the Word

31-Day Devotional
by
Dick Mills

Day 1

**And your feet shod with the preparation
of the gospel of peace.
Ephesians 6:15**

The ability to remain on one's feet during battle requires good footing, strong ankle action and proper footwear. This expression, "your feet shod with the *preparation* of the gospel of peace," says a lot. The original Greek word translated **preparation** in this verse is *hetoimasia (het-oy-mas-eé-ah)*. It is defined as "being ready to take action at a moment's notice."

This is a word that is both defensive and offensive. In Roman times, the warrior's sandal was equipped with a cleat-like sole for sure traction and fast mobility. Taking the gospel to the ends of the earth stirs up opposition. The enemy's strategy is to aim his artillery at us to stop our forward progress. Being shod with the warrior's sandal of readiness will assure us of the steadfast footing and nimble agility necessary to dodge Satan's missiles.

We can also launch an offensive attack when shod with this footwear. The New Testament usage of the word *hetoimasia* implies a readiness for good works (Titus 3:1), a readiness for witnessing (1 Pet. 3:15), and a readiness for the Lord's return. (Matt. 24:44.) Such readiness imparts to us a distinctive character and nature because at any moment we expect a triumphant return of our Commander-in-Chief. Readiness also keeps us open to the demands of the action necessary to reach our goal of world dominion.

Shod with the right kind of combat sandal we are able to defend ourselves. We are also equipped to launch a worldwide invasion of the kingdom of darkness.

Day 2

**The Lord is my shepherd.
Nothing shall be lacking to me.
Psalm 23:1 (author's literal translation)**

This is a security verse. Safe in the shepherd's fold we know no lack, no want, no deficiency, no shortage. Psalm 84:11 assures us: **. . . no good thing will he withhold from them that walk uprightly.** In Psalm 34:9 we are told: **O, fear the Lord, ye His saints: there is no want to them that fear him.**

One way a shepherd tends his flock is by seeing that they have good nourishing food. As our Divine Shepherd, the Lord wants us to have a healthy diet. The Word of God is one source of spiritual nourishment. Worship of the Lord is another. Inspired and anointed teaching and preaching is food for the soul. Our Shepherd will supply to us just the right nourishment, if we will let Him, if we will follow Him in obedience.

A shepherd also protects his flock. We can trust our keeping to our Chief Shepherd, Jesus, Who will not leave us open to the enemy's designs. Our protection, our safety, our preservation, our care, and our safekeeping are all His personal concerns. We believers are ever under His watchful eye. Jesus protects the flock from marauders. He has given to His undershepherds (pastors) an admonition to keep the wolves out of His sheepfold.

A shepherd continuously leads his flock to better pasture. Our Chief Shepherd is constantly looking out for our best interests. He only wants for us what is for our ultimate good.

Day 2

Saying "The Lord is *my* Shepherd" personalizes this statement. To proclaim "I shall not lack or want" is to declare that, as one of the Lord's followers, each of us is supplied and contented in every way.

Day 3

. . . And be not conformed to this world, but be ye transformed by the renewing of your mind. . . .
Romans 12:2

A lady came home from a revival meeting and cheerfully announced to her agnostic husband, "I have been born again." In contempt he snarled these words at her: "You have lost your mind!" She lovingly responded, "You're right! Now I have the mind of Christ." She was sharing with him that her whole way of thinking had been changed as a result of her conversion.

One of the key words in this verse is **transformed.** In the original Greek text it is *metamorphoo (met-am-or-fó-o).* The interesting thing about *metamorphoo* is that it is the same word used to describe the change Jesus underwent going up the mount of transfiguration. (Matt. 17:2.)

As Jesus ascended the mountain, His clothing became as white as light and His face shone with a dazzling glory as bright as the sun. He was transfigured *(metamorphoo)* or transformed. What happened to Jesus was a drastic and dramatic change from His former condition. Here in Romans, Paul is urging you and me to undergo the same process.

In 2 Corinthians 3:18 Paul writes: **But we all, with open face beholding as in a glass the glory of the Lord, are changed into the same image from glory to glory, even as by the Spirit of the Lord.**

The radiance Jesus demonstrated on the mount of transfiguration is resident within us by the indwelling Spirit of God. As our hearts and minds respond to His dealing, we, too, are being transfigured or transformed.

Day 4

**Many are the afflictions of the righteous:
but the Lord delivereth him out of them all.
Psalm 34:19**

This verse is not declaring that you and I are going to suffer all our lives. There is no redemptive value in suffering; it entered the world as a result of sin not as a "cure" for it. Sin and suffering are two ominous figures that have dogged the footsteps of humanity ever since the fall of man. Jesus came to do away with sin and suffering.

Job's suffering was labeled a "captivity" from which he was released by God. (Job 42:10.) The woman with a crooked, deformed back was pronounced by Jesus as one "whom Satan hath bound." (Luke 13:16.) In Acts 10:38 we read **How God anointed Jesus of Nazareth with the Holy Ghost and with power: who went about doing good, and healing all that were oppressed of the devil....** This word translated **oppressed** could also be rendered **tyrannized**. When the Bible describes afflictions as captivity, bondage, oppression, and tyranny, then we are safe in saying that suffering has no redemptive value.

In the Greek Old Testament (LXX), this word **afflictions** is *thlipsis* (thlip'-sis) which is defined as "pressure."

Many are the pressures of the righteous. We are on an uphill journey, an obstacle course. Every turn in the road is a pressure point. The Lord delivers us out of them all and we manage to keep going. Do not major on the pressure points of life; rather, major on deliverance. Negative people are always talking about their afflictions and pressures. Positive people of faith are always talking about their deliverances.

Day 5

. . . to another faith. . . .
1 Corinthians 12:9

This verse refers to the gift of faith that God has for each of us to equip us for any special need that may arise in our life. One translator calls it "heroic faith." Another scholar calls it "wonder-working faith." This promise lets us know that we do not have to be anxious or insecure about the days to come. Some people dread the uncertain future and are tense and nervous as they look ahead to tomorrow. Some carry on as though the fuse has been lit and now we are waiting for the bomb to go off.

The gift of faith is special to the occasion. It rests in the confidence that Jesus is the same yesterday, today, and forever. (Heb. 13:8.) The gift of faith confidently states: "God has met us in the past, He is meeting us in the present, and we know He will still meet us in the future. He brought us out to bring us in. He has brought us this far and He will see us through." (2 Cor. 1:10.) When the Lord imparts this gift of special faith to us, great peace and inward calm comes to our soul. Our spirit confidently proclaims to us: "It shall be well with you." (Is. 3:10.)

Aren't you glad the future is all known to the Lord? Aren't you glad the steps of the righteous are ordered by the Lord? (Ps. 37:23.) For all emergencies and special times of need that may arise, He has the gift of "special" faith just for you. It is the God-given ability to trust your situation into His hands and see Him work it out for your comfort and for His glory. Special faith is yours for the asking!

Day 6

**To him that overcometh will I grant to sit
with me in my throne . . . .
Revelation 3:21**

In the book of Revelation, each of the seven churches in Asia is promised a different reward for overcoming the flesh, the world and the devil. These rewards include the privilege of eating of the tree of life and the hidden manna, power over the nations, being clothed in white raiment, and being made a pillar in the temple of God. The last church mentioned was Laodicea. The reward offered them was this promise to be enthroned with Jesus in a place of glory and honor.

There are many similarities between the tendencies of the Laodiceans and the modern-day Church. Their lukewarmness, complacency, smugness, and spiritual conceit are characteristics we see prevalent in many of our churches today.

I used to think the grestest rewards were reserved for the martyrs. Surely, I thought, giving up one's life for the cause of Christ would bring great rewards. Second on my reward list were the missionaries. If anybody deserved special rewards for self-sacrifice, doubtless it was this group of brave people who had given up everything to go witness to foreign people.

But the truth is, the greatest reward is promised to those who can keep a zeal alive, a flame of devotion, and a spiritual intensity in a world filled with apathy and spiritual indifference. Keeping the fire of the Holy Ghost burning in the midst of ineptitude, mediocrity, and spiritual lethargy results in the privilege of sitting on the throne with Jesus.

Day 7

**Wisdom and knowledge shall be
the stability of thy times....
Isaiah 33:6**

Wisdom and knowledge go together like a husband and wife. They dovetail.

Knowledge is facts; it is informational. Wisdom is understanding; it is directive, procedural. Knowledge provides the data needed to be informed and aware. Wisdom provides the insight necessary to know how to proceed based on the facts at hand. For example, Noah had the facts about the coming worldwide flood 120 years before it arrived on the scene. But he really didn't know what to do about that flood until a word of wisdom came to him saying, "Build an ark."

You and I can be intuitively and sensitively cognizant of coming events in our own life. But knowledge alone is not enough. We need to wait for wisdom to show us how to proceed. James tells us that if anyone lacks wisdom, it is available for the asking.

Lot and Abraham both knew that Sodom was going to end up at the bottom of the Dead Sea. Abraham knew it a week before it happened, and Lot knew it a day ahead of time. To those who are truly in tune with the Lord, knowledge always comes first because God is omniscient; He knows *all* things. Proverbs 14:6 says that knowledge is **easy** to the person who understands. There is not anything the Lord doesn't know. He even invites His children to be curious enough about their future to ask Him about it. (Jer. 33:3.) Once we have done that, once we

Day 7

have the facts, then we are to inquire and ask for wisdom and direction. With both wisdom *and* knowledge, we are standing on solid ground.

Day 8

... for the iniquity of the Amorites is not yet full.
Genesis 15:16

Here the Lord is telling Abraham that occupancy of the land promised to his descendants can only take place when the depravity of the Amorites who live there has reached its zenith. This event took place over 400 years later. The land literally vomited out the Amorites because of their total degeneracy and depravity. It was then that Israel was able to go in and possess the land as their inheritance.

This event explains why the Lord Jesus has not yet returned to the earth. Over 318 verses in the New Testament point to Christ's Second Coming. Right now we are seeing all the malignant forces of evil heading towards a culmination of total depravity. This action will produce the man of sin — the antichrist. He will be spawned in a garbage-can society that reeks of filth and degradation.

At the same time all this is taking place, a work of righteousness is being developed and orchestrated in God's people. The loving, compassionate nature of Christ is being implanted and formed in our hearts. Hate in the world is making the sinners more like Satan. Love in the Christians is making us more like Jesus. Earthly, sensual and devilish wisdom is fully demonstrated in Satan's followers. The pure and holy wisdom from above is conspicuous in the followers of Jesus. When the iniquity of the latter-day Amorites reaches its saturation point, the righteousness of the bride of Christ will produce the Second Coming of Jesus. (Rev. 19:7.)

Day 9

> ... the people that do know their God
> shall be strong, and do exploits.
> **Daniel 11:32**

This verse covers life during times of great stress, pressure, and turmoil. It is not speaking of a time of unparalleled peace, prosperity, and plenty. It is a promise that shows us how to survive in a climate of international tension, economic upheaval, and spiritual change. This word from the Lord tells us that persecution of the Christians will result in greater knowledge ("they shall know their God"), greater strength ("they shall be strong"), and greater miracles ("they shall do exploits"). The more difficult the days, the greater God's power will be demonstrated. You and I should be encouraged knowing that the Lord is fortifying us for the future. We are not only going to survive, we have been promised that miracles will accompany our Christian witness.

In times of great opposition to the Church of the living God, the world becomes a combat zone between God and Satan. Where sin abounds, grace abounds even more. (Rom. 5:20.) The greater the darkness, the greater the light. Right in the midst of the devil's revival of occultism and mystic religions, the Holy Ghost is being poured out in copious measure.

The Church of Jesus Christ is not getting weaker and weaker as the end of time approaches; it is getting stronger and stronger. We believers are going out in a blaze of glory. We will know the Lord intimately, have a prevailing strength, and do notable feats and miracles in His name! Our future prospect is victory all the way!

Day 10

**Because they have no changes,
therefore they fear not God.
Psalm 55:19**

How resistant to change are you? How much pain does a new idea cause you? How willing are you to discard a method that no longer works, a tradition that has lost its meaning, a methodology that has become ineffective? Would you agree with the statement that sameness begets tameness, and tameness begets lameness?

Changes do not come easily to any of us. Especially to those in the church world. But change we must, because of the condition of the lost and needy world. The unsaved world is rushing downhill to eternity. It is going to take something drastic to catch their attention and stem the tide of this self-destructing society in which we live. To refuse to adapt to changing circumstances is to ignore the cries for help of a lost society. Being locked into our traditional ways of doing things could keep us from a readiness to respond to the calls for help that our lost world keeps sending forth.

The verse for today says that if you and I will not change, it is because tradition means more to us than the reverential fear of the Lord. You and I have a lot of reasons for not changing, but our God wants us to trust Him completely for the future and allow Him to make any necessary adjustments. Such trust qualifies us for the capacity of reverentially fearing the Lord.

Day 11

**But the path of the just is as the shining light,
that shineth more and more unto the perfect day.
Proverbs 4:18**

One time my dad and I went hiking all night in the Sierras. We parked the car at a trail head and began an eight-mile hike by flashlight into the back country. Between 4 and 5 a.m. a transition began to take place. All the nocturnal activity terminated. Although we were in an area populated by marauding bears, stealthy mountain lions, howling timber wolves, and barking coyotes, everything became unearthly quiet. Total silence settled over the forest. It was as though the stalking creatures had retired to their lairs and dens and gone to sleep. There was not yet any light so the daytime creatures were still inactive. There was an indescribable hush which lasted for about an hour. Then about 5 a.m. the first ray of light appeared over the horizon.

From that moment on, the forest gradually became a bedlam of noise from chipmunks, stellar jays, golden mantled ground squirrels, quail, and other chattering creatures. By the time the full rays of sun finally broke through the heavy foliage about 6 a.m., the forest was alive with the vibrant sounds of life.

This verse tells us that our Christian journey is like that time just before the sunrise. The night is far spent and the day is at hand. (Rom. 13:12.) For the believer, the long dark night is being replaced by a new day at which time **. . . shall the Sun of righteousness arise with healing in his wings** (Mal. 4:2). His glory shall light up the earth. For us who believe, it is getting brighter and brighter!

Day 12

**My glory was fresh in me,
and my bow was renewed in my hand.
Job 29:20**

The bow represented the livelihood of ancient peoples. Not only was it used for military purposes, but also to obtain wild animals for food. In other words, early people lived by the bow. For it to be renewed in the hand meant that the archer was getting stronger and stronger. This verse is thus an assurance that we can function in life and not be fatigued in our everyday activities. We can be refreshed as we go about doing God's will.

Stringing the bow took a great deal of exertion and energy. When not in use, it would be left unstrung because it was discovered that a bow left strung up would lose its tensile strength and elasticity. We derive our word *dente* from this concept of a bow being unstrung. You can readily see that in primitive times stringing and unstringing the bow would be a time-consuming and strenuous exercise. Job is telling us here that ordinarily he would be completely worn out when doing his normal work. Instead, God's glory and honor refreshed him, and his bow was renewed or changed in his hand. As a result, he did not get weaker and weaker, but stronger and stronger.

Use your faith and you will get more faith. Use your strength for the Lord and He will give you more strength. Give joy to others and God will replace it with more joy. Impart courage and courage will be imparted to you. Give and it shall be given. Getting stronger while exerting energy may seem a reversal of the natural order, but it is a spiritual truth from which we can all benefit.

Day 13

Call unto me, and I will answer thee, and shew thee great and mighty things, which thou knowest not.
Jeremiah 33:3

One post-war development of which we are all aware are the giant underground missile silos.

The Hebrew word translated **mighty** in this verse implies the same kind of invisible sources of power. It has to do with the hidden, the inaccessible, that which is subliminal or below the surface of normal vision. This promise reassures us that if we will but call upon the Lord, He will bring such things into the scope of our vision: "I will show you great and fortified things that up to now have escaped your attention."

While I was in the service, the Lord began dealing with me about forgiving a sergeant who had been making my life miserable. My chief concern at the moment was an overdue auto payment. The Lord was zeroing in on my need to forgive while I was concentrating on a threat by the bank to repossess the car. In keeping with my priority list, I kept insisting in prayer that the Lord help me with the car, and then we could discuss the sergeant. God conveyed to me that top priority was an act of genuine forgiveness on my part. Once that issue was settled, then we could talk about the car payment.

The Lord won out. I had a beautiful release of love, joy, and peace as true forgiveness came. At that time, a family member called my attention to a letter on my dresser. It contained more than enough money to make the car payment. The sobering fact surfaced that the letter had

Day 13

been lying there for three days unnoticed. God is thus saying to us here: "Your answer is there; call upon Me, and I will make it visible to you."

Day 14

*. . . I have loved thee with an everlasting love:
therefore with lovingkindness have I drawn thee.*
Jeremiah 31:3

Have you ever seen the letters TLC written on a bedside hospital chart? This symbol is used to tell all personnel that this patient needs a lot of "tender loving care." This verse in Jeremiah lets us know that TLC originated with the Lord: "I have loved you with an *everlasting* love," He says. This is an eternal love. It never oscillates, vacillates, or fluctuates. It does not freeze over in winter or dry up in summer. It is constant and perennial.

How often we encounter conditional love. Our society is structured on it. We soon get the message: "If you want to be accepted, measure up." Conditional love sets achievement levels and goals that are usually beyond reach. It forces us to compete for acceptance, approval or affection. Such competition produces alienation. One person wins the prize, the rest are losers who must learn to cope with rejection.

God has an unconditional love for us. He does not love us *because* we are somebody; He loves us so we will *become* somebody. He loves each of us as though there were no one else to love but us. He will never love us a bit more in the future than He loves us right now. We can grieve the Lord, insult Him, resist Him, and even disobey Him. None of these things removes or lessens His love. Our perverse actions only hinder His blessings, because God can only bless obedience. But we cannot add to God's love or subtract from it. The good news is that we can cooperate with His love and enjoy it forever.

The message is: God loves *you.*

Day 15

**Do not remember the former things,
neither consider the things of old. Behold,
I will do a new thing; now it shall spring forth....**
Isaiah 43:18,19

Former things are those that have occurred during the last few years... recent things or things that are still fresh in our memory... those things people talk about for days afterwards. They seem to be conversation pieces. This verse challenges us to turn 180 degrees and start planning for a good future.

Things of old go back in time... back to antiquity. History, tradition, and past ages can be included in these things of old. The verse commands us to leave the past and get ready for the future. The Lord has new things for us. It is impossible to look in two directions at the same time. Clinging to past memories could cause us to pass up the new things and miss out altogether on good things He has planned for us.

A new thing is exciting. It refers to something fresh, exciting and exhilarating rather than predictable, lackluster, dull, boring, or routine. The Lord promises to put us on a daily diet of challenges all to stimulate and build our faith. Each day can be another unfolding of the divine drama in our life.

Now it shall spring forth. This phrase **spring forth** means the same as *to sprout*. It refers to a plant growing out of the ground. God's Word is a seed planted in the heart. Faith causes it to germinate and sprout. The end result is fruitfulness. Instead of living in the past, you and I can now lead fruitful, productive lives.

Day 16

... then thou shalt have good success.
Joshua 1:8

Success is a Bible word. As the power center of the universe, Jesus is a success with a capital S. He was a success in the dawn of time when an enemy tried to unseat Him from His throne of authority. (Is. 14:12-15.) He was a success in the Garden of Eden when the messianic promise was given concerning the defeat of Satan's realm. (Gen. 3:15.) He succeeded at the crucifixion and at the resurrection. (1 John 3:8; Col. 2:14,15.) He will succeed at the Second Coming, on the day of judgment (Phil. 2:10,11), and in eternity.

Serving the Lord lines a person up with the victorious cause — past, present, and future. Joshua 1:8 tells us that by following the Lord you and I will make our way prosperous and experience good success. God's standards for evaluating success are even higher than those established by man. The original Hebrew word translated **success** in this verse is *sakal (saw-kal')*. Besides indicating the ability to accomplish or achieve some goal, *sakal* includes the possession of discretion, intelligence, prudence, wisdom, and good understanding.

We attribute success to winning athletes, popularly elected politicians, self-made millionaires, and all kinds of achievers. The Biblical principles of success are built on faithfulness, trust, integrity, discipline, and obedience. When you and I are promised success in Joshua 1:8, we are assured of arriving at our destination safe and sound. We are also assured of the expertise and ability to achieve our goals. We succeed not only in reaching our objectives, but also in the methods chosen to attain those high ideals.

Day 17

. . . he that believeth shall not make haste.
Isaiah 28:16

It is too late in the day for rash action. You and I have been serving the Lord too long to begin making snap judgments, jumping to conclusions, or becoming impulsive. This promise is an assurance that we can avoid the mistakes that come from impatience or acting on impulse.

If you have a history of precipitating crises by acting too hastily, would not this be a good day to begin overcoming that tendency? Remember: "He that believes shall not make haste."

One of the things that helped me in this area was the discovery that most of my hasty acts occurred because I did not have all the facts. Later, after all the needed information has surfaced, then I regretted my premature action. In 1 Corinthians 4:5 the Apostle Paul encourages us to . . . **judge nothing before the time.** . . . Then we will be fully cognizant of what is going on and we can act with confidence and assurance.

Another cause of hasty action is frustration. We would like to see things happen. Everything seems to be standing still. We get impatient. We feel that a slight nudge will get things rolling. We try to hurry up God's plan. In so doing we create a new set of problems. This verse was placed in the Bible just for those of us who could easily take things into our own hands and try to "get on with it" — only to botch things up worse than if we had done nothing at all.

Day 17

Note Psalm 37:5: **Commit thy way unto the Lord, trust also in him; and he shall bring it to pass.** You might want to add these three verses to your active vocabulary. If so, do it today.

Day 18

And my people shall dwell in a peaceable habitation, and in sure dwellings, and in quiet resting places.
Isaiah 32:18

Have you ever walked into a home and felt peace and serenity? Have you ever been in a home that gave you a feeling of turmoil, confusion, or even hostility? A home will take on the very nature of its residents. Disciplined and well-adjusted families give a home the feeling of teamwork and harmony. A home filled with bickering and strife exudes a spirit of tension and dissension. A home in which love resides reflects an atmosphere of peace and joy.

This verse promises peace, security, and tranquillity. Since we are called God's people, it is reasonable to expect His attributes to be demonstrated in our lives and in our homes. Since God is not the author of confusion, but of peace, we can believe for peace to rule and reign in our homes.

Our God also promises us sure or secure dwellings. I believe we can claim a good foundation for our natural homes. Security is assured us against flood, fire, earthquake, tornado, hurricane, or any other natural disturbance.

We know the world is full of potential natural disasters. We also know the Word of God promises us a secure dwelling. I would rather stand on God's promises and be secure than to allow the fears generated by the news media to dominate my life and make me feel insecure.

Day 19

*... When the enemy shall come in like a flood, the
Spirit of the Lord shall lift up a standard against him.*
Isaiah 59:19

The original Hebrew word translated **standard** in this verse in *nuwc (noos)*. It is an unusual word signifying something displayed in order to put to flight or to chase away oppositions so that a person can escape or be delivered. The Spirit of the Lord will lift up a standard *(nuwc)* not only to turn back the floodtide of the enemy that comes against us, but also to deliver us and give us a way of escape. Our God not only promises to stop the opposition in its tracks, but to show us the way through to our next point of victory.

The image *nuwc* gives is that of a brake and an accelerator on an automobile. The Lord tells us that He will put the brakes on the enemy and at the same time will accelerate our forward progress. The enemy will go back to his starting place, turned back by the Spirit of God. We, on the other hand, will get on with living. We will be set free to go ahead and fulfill the will and call of God on our life. Satan goes backward while we go forward. This exchange puts us way ahead of the opposition and the competition.

Isaiah referred to **. . . them that turn the battle to the gate** (Is. 28:6). As in the expression "the gates of hell" (Matt. 16:18), this alludes to the place from which Satan's malignant forces issue. To "turn the battle to the gate" is to drive Satan back to his starting place. This action frees us to get on with our journey, to press on to even greater levels of victory and triumph in Christ.

Day 20

And when they began to sing and to praise, the Lord set ambushes against the children. . . which were come against Judah; and they were smitten.
2 Chronicles 20:22

Think of it! Singing and praising your way to victory. Singing and praising your way through discouragement, oppression, depression, fear, and worry.

. . . and they were three days in gathering of the spoil, (the loot) **it was so much** (v. 25). In Bible days, driving an enemy out entitled the victor to all the spoils of battle. The army of Judah so routed the enemy that it took them three days to collect all the booty the enemy had left behind. And the victory was wrought not by fighting but by singing and praising the Lord!

God responded to the prayers of His people with these reassuring words: **. . . the battle is not yours, but God's** (v. 15). With this assurance, the king of Judah appointed singers and praisers to go out before the army and to praise the Lord. When they began to sing and praise, the enemy was defeated. They key word in this passage is **began.** Your victory is dependent upon your doing something. You need to *begin.* To begin to count your blessings. To begin to emulate past deliverances. To begin to praise the Lord. To begin to sing your song of deliverance.

The Bible says that the Lord inhabits the praises of His people. (Ps. 22:3.) When the Lord's presence comes into our setting of praise and worship, the enemy is powerless against us. We can literally sing our way through every

Day 20

battle and win the victory the same way Jehoshaphat's army won. Singing and praising the Lord is an effective weapon in our spiritual warfare!

Day 21

**And shall make him of quick understanding
in the fear of the Lord....**
Isaiah 11:3

In the original Hebrew this expression **quick understanding** is "quick scented." It is the Hebrew word for spirit, *ruwach (roó-akh)* which has to do with breathing, respiration, perceiving by scent or smell, discerning by aroma, or detecting by breath. It is the ability to detect, judge, and determine a thing by the way it smells. Thus, "quick understanding" is equal to instantaneous discernment by the sense of smell.

All living organisms have a distinctive fragrance or aroma. It is the breath of life. Everything God touches comes alive and emits the aroma of life. Everything Satan touches dies and produces the aroma of death. Everything the unregenerated human spirit (or man in his natural state) touches gives forth the aroma of his perspiration (his ego-drive). So, three distinct aromas can be detected for discerning purposes: 1) The perfume that accompanies and identifies the true worship of God in spirit and in truth, 2) the stench of death that is evidence of Satan at work, and 3) the smell of human perspiration produced by man in his own self-efforts. To have "quick understanding: or to be "quick scented" in the things of life means that we are able to instantly discern what is happening, to know what is behind every activity with which we come in contact. What a blessing to be spiritually *scent*-sitive!

Day 22

Beloved, I wish above all things that thou mayest prosper and be in health, even as thy soul prospereth.
3 John 2

In Greek the word translated **health** in this verse is *hugiaino (hoog-ee-ah´ee-no)* from which we derive our English word *hygiene*. It is defined as "sound," "healthy," "free from disease or void of the germs that cause sickness and disability."

This wish by John was expressed to a man named Gaius who worried himself sick over his problems. John was sending traveling ministers to Gaius' church. An influential member of that church by the name of Diotrephes did not want these ministers to come so he vigorously opposed the plan, apparently threatening to cut off his financial support if it was carried out. Gaius was thus caught in the middle.

This verse is part of John's letter written in response to the situation. In it, John is telling Gaius: "Look, you do not need to worry over this situation. Diotrephes does not have all the money in the world. He is causing problems because he loves to have pre-eminence. But, Gaius, God wants you to look to Him as your sole source of supply. I am praying that you will prosper financially, and be in health, even as your soul prospers."

Hugiaino is used for sound doctrine and sound teaching. Your body is the temple of the Holy Ghost. You are storing in it massive amounts of the Word of God. That Word is sound and healthy. You can do more for the Lord with a healthy body than with a sick one. A sound and healthy body is the ideal receptacle for the sound and healthy scriptures which you have hid in your heart.

Day 23

...taking the shield of faith...
to quench all the fiery darts of the wicked.
Ephesians 6:16

Crimes of passion take place when the enemy ignites an inflammable area within the human personality. We hear of flaming anger, fiery jealousy, burning passion, of people being afire with lust, consumed by hatred, devoured by the flames of prejudice. All these can occur when a person has no guard to protect him from the fiery darts of Satan.

The word *diaballo* (the original Greek word for the devil) is composed of two words: *dia* meaning "through" and *ballo* meaning "to throw." *Diaballo* is thus the evil one who tries to throw fiery darts through the believer. These darts will ignite trouble in some area of life if a shield is not used. In Roman days the shield was as big as a door. With it a soldier could advance under attack knowing that he had no vulnerable areas exposed.

As mature Christian soldiers we are called out of the comfort zone into the combat zone, out of the nursery into the trenches. We are to get off the charismatic love boat where life has been all fun and games and onto a spiritual battleship from which we can shell the enemy's fortresses and demolish his strongholds.

The shield of faith enables us to remain unscathed in the very midst of battle while the onslaught is at its worst. No area of our life or personality can be touched. The shield of faith completely covers every area of our existence. We are not only protected, we are gaining ground against our adversary. The Church of God is moving onward to greater victories.

Day 24

> ... make not provision for the flesh,
> to fulfill the lusts thereof.
> **Romans 13:14**

You have doubtless heard the old saying: "People do not plan to fail, they just fail to plan." This verse addresses those who actually do plan to fail. They work failure into their confession, their plans, their expectancy. You can hear it in their conversation: "If this marriage doesn't work, I can always get a divorce." "If the business goes under, I can always file bankruptcy." "If the Lord doesn't heal me, I can always use Blue Cross and Medicare." Such words are more than attempts to plan for contingencies, they are actually attempts to justify failure before it ever happens.

In Romans 13:14 the Apostle Paul warns against such pre-planned failure. He tells us in essence: "Don't work failure into your plans. Don't allow for it. Don't even put it on the agenda."

Provision is an interesting word. In the original Greek it is *pronoia (pron'-oy-ah)*. *Pro* is a prefix meaning "before, in front of, prior to, ahead of time" (compare prologue — words spoken before the main dissertation). *Noia* comes from *noieo* referring to the mind, perception, the intellect, the thought. Thus, *provision (pronoia)* is thinking about something ahead of time. People plan their vacations, their holidays, their income tax filings, and a myriad other happenings during the course of a year. That is good — if it's positive. Negative planning is disastrous.

Don't plan on bankruptcy. Don't plan on trouble. Don't plan on losing your temper. No general ever goes out to

Day 24

battle planning on losing. Plan on winning. Plan on victory. It is in Christ. It is in this verse.

Day 25

And great earthquakes shall be in divers places. . . .
Luke 21:11

Revivals seem to parallel natural phenomena. Occurrences in the natural world are usually accompanied by similar events in the spiritual world. The San Francisco earthquake happened at the same time that the Welsh revival and the pentecostal outpouring were taking place in 1906. Natural shaking and spiritual shaking go together.

In our verse in Luke, we are told of great earthquakes which will happen all over the world in the last days. Haggai 2:6 tells us that heaven, earth, the sea, and the dry land will be shaken and God's house will be filled with glory. In Ezekiel's valley of dry bones, a shaking took place as bone was knit to bone. In the days of Uzziah, king of Judah, a great earthquake occurred. We read in Amos 1:1 that recorded time is built around events happening prior to the earthquake. When Moses received the Ten Commandments, the mountain quaked. When Jesus died on the cross, the whole world shook. On resurrection morning another earthquake took place. Hebrews 12:26,27 promises that prior to the coming of the Lord Jesus there will be more earthquakes.

Perhaps reading prophesies about the earth shaking is not your way to start the new day. But with the natural goes the supernatural. The good news is, "The Lord is stirring His people." His Church is being jolted out of her lethargy. Old antiquated and obsolete traditions are being shaken to the very foundations. This shaking has to take place before we will accept the new things God has in store for us.

Day 26

... see if there be any wicked way in me....
Psalm 139:24

In the Greek Old Testament (LXX), the word translated **wicked** here is *kakos (kak-os´)* meaning "ill." David is praying for the Lord to check him over to see how spiritually healthy he is. He is saying to the Lord: "How about my attitude? Do I harbor resentment? Is there repressed anger lurking inside of me? Do imaginations and fantasy dominate my thinking? Do hurts, real or imagined, constantly occur?" By asking the Lord to make a spiritual x-ray of his inner man, David is risking the pain and embarrassment of being found guilty of hidden and presumptuous sins. Can we take the same risk and ask the Lord for His inspection?

Man has explored everything but the explorer himself. He has climbed all the mountains of the world, but has not penetrated or searched out all the ridges of his own heart. Jeremiah labored with this truth when he posed the classic question: **The heart is deceitful above all things, and desperately wicked** (Heb., *anach*, "sick"); **who can know it?** (Jer. 17:9). In the very next verse, the Lord responds rapidly with these reassuring words: **I the Lord search the heart, I try the reins, even to give every man according to his ways, and according to the fruit of his doings.**

Heart searching is painful, but it is part of the purifying, purging, pruning, perfecting, and polishing process designed by the Lord to bring us to full maturity in Christ. It is possible to approach the Lord with "clean hands and a pure heart," but it does take total honesty and a commitment to truth that will not allow us to hide anything in our heart that displeases the Lord.

Day 27

**O Lord, correct me, but with judgment;
not in thine anger, lest thou bring me to nothing.
Jeremiah 10:24**

Take a lump of clay or a clod of earth. Tell this muddy mass that there is a chance that he can be worked over, improved upon, changed, remade, and then fashioned after the very nature of the Designer Who created him in the first place. Call this process re-creation, regeneration, or rebirth. Then show him the majestic qualities of the Architect. Tell him that he can be just like that. Tell him it is a lifetime process, but the end result is being conformed to the image of his Savior and Lord. That earthly person is going to respond very favorably. Some people may think it too good to be true, but most will think it worth striving for. From the earthly first Adam to the heavenly second Adam is quite a journey. The long-suffering God waits patiently while the corrective work is going on.

In this verse Jeremiah, acknowledging his need for adjustment, fine tuning, finishing, and correcting, asks the Lord to remove carnality and replace it with spirituality. He knows it will take time so he asks the Lord to be patient with him. Jeremiah is negotiating with the Lord. He tells Him he needs correction (who doesn't?). He asks the Lord for justice. He wants to be right. He wants the truth. He wants to be totally honest. He appeals to the mercy side of the Lord. So can you. Ask the Lord to give you a heart after Him and inclined toward Him. His attribute of mercy will permeate you, for to the merciful He will show mercy.

Day 28

. . . faint, yet pursuing. . . .
Judges 8:4

Athletes claim that fatigue can improve their performance. Getting tired during the contest moves them from reason to instinct. They accomplish things in their automatic output of energy they would not be able to do if they were figuring things out mentally.

"Faint, yet pursuing" is used to describe the condition of the three hundred men assigned by God to Gideon to fight Israel's battles for her. The enemy was being routed and put to fight. In order to capture them, Gideon's little army, hungry and tired as they were, had no choice but to continue pursuit. Smelling victory and tasting success, they were highly motivated to carry on. They were willing to forego the usual eating and sleeping schedule in order to press the battle to the gates. (Is. 28:6.) This is a message to intercessors as well as soulwinners.

There are times in our lives when we need Gideon's mentality. Sometimes we, too, are exhausted but still in pursuit with victory in sight, the enemy on the run, and a few extra hours needed to wrap things up. This does not mean that we advocate a disregard for proper rest and nourishment. Many articles have been written about revival that ended prematurely because the participants ignored the body's natural need for food and rest. Breaking laws of health is not the way to win spiritual battles. "Faint, yet pursuing" does reveal how the thrill of conquest, the assurance of victory, and the joy of knowing we are winning in the contest against our enemy will spur us on. This spiritual "second wind" is a priority item to the Christian.

Day 29

... Let not him that girdeth on his harness boast himself as he that putteth it off.
1 Kings 20:11

The one who takes his armor off is the tried, tested, seasoned veteran who has been in battle and lived to tell about it. He has learned to survive. He understands his opponent. He knows the stratagems, designs, ruses, and cunning of the enemy. He has also found from his battle experiences that as tough as his adversary may be, he is vulnerable and can be defeated. The one taking off the armor has a victory to report. He has earned the respect of his fellow soldiers by helping the cause of truth to gain new footholds and win new ground. He could write the manual of fighting and winning. He also keeps the victory in right perspective. He knows all triumph is a result of teamwork. A true hero wisely recognizes that victory is always the fruit of combined effort. He takes the armor off as a real winner, humbly grateful to be alive.

The one who puts on the armor (for the first time) is a rookie. Inexperienced, untested, unproven, full of enthusiasm, and even a little conceited: "Let me at 'em; just wait till I get into combat, I'll show 'em a thing or two." These are invariably the words of the one putting on the armor. Such bravado is rarely heard issuing from the mouth of the veteran. It is typical of the untried youth full of his own eagerness and supposed prowess. Soon enough his boasting will be replaced by a more sober, mature viewpoint. The one who takes off the armor has a different attitude from the one who puts it on.

Day 30

He stretcheth out the north over the empty space....
Job 26:7

It has been conjectured that in our universe there is an area to the north of our earth in which there are no stars, planet, or other heavenly bodies. It is supposed to be sort of a void, an empty nothingness. Along with this "empty north" verse in Job, there is a statement in Isaiah 14:13 about Lucifer aspiring to sit in control ... **upon the mount of the congregation in the sides of the north.** Apparently the Lord announced in the dawn of time that the north was empty on purpose, it was destined to be filled with a congregation of worshippers. In Psalm 48:2, Mount Zion is identified as being ... **on the sides of the north.** ... Zion is always symbolic of the place where true worshipers gather together to celebrate the Lord's name.

John the revelator saw something that could be a fulfillment of these verses. In Revelation 21:2 he writes: **I John saw the holy city, new Jerusalem, coming down from God out of heaven, prepared as a bride adorned for her husband.** Here we have the potential for full drama: 1) At creation God deliberately leaves a square slot in the universe with nothing in it. 2) He announces that this space is reserved for a future bride for His Son. This bride will be a large number of people. They will make up the congregation in the mount on the farthest sides of the north. The empty north will soon be occupied. The void place will be filled in with the redeemed. This is the true dignity and destiny God offers to the human race!

Day 31

**And God hath set... in the church...
helps, governments....
1 Corinthians 12:28**

According to the usual interpretation of this verse, **helps** refers to those people in the church who serve as deacons and deaconesses, along with the other unpaid, volunteer workers who assist the employed staff members who occupy positions of leadership. **Governments** are the church administrators, those on the payroll, the titled staff. Thus, as a rule, helps and governments are assumed to describe officers in the church and those who assist them. However, there are some options that are worth considering.

J. R. Pridie wrote a book (circa 1926) on the healing ministries of the church. In this book he suggested that governments could be interpreted to include words of knowledge and wisdom, as well as the discernment, diagnosis and treatment of sickness. Likewise, **helps** was translated "nursing" or any beneficial acts aimed at helping a sick person to recover or mend. It is very interesting that helps and governments in the text occur right after the phrase **gifts** (plural) **of healing**. It is as though these two words, helps and governments, are an extension of the healing ministries.

I visualize one team having a capacity to minister to the sick with revelation knowledge, compassionate words of wisdom, a penetrating discernment that sees the cause of the sickness, knowing how to get to the root of the problem and even being able to minister healing to the person in

Day 31

need. Then the helps ministry would step in and begin nursing the person to spiritual health, stamina and vitality. Any volunteers for these ministries?

Reading the Bible in One Year

JANUARY

1 Gen. 1-2; Ps.1; Matt. 1-2
2 Gen. 3-4; Ps. 2; Matt. 3-4
3 Gen. 5-7; Ps. 3; Matt. 5
4 Gen. 8-9; Ps. 4; Matt. 6-7
5 Gen. 10-11; Ps. 5; Matt. 8-9
6 Gen. 12-13; Ps. 6; Matt. 10-11
7 Gen. 14-15; Ps. 7; Matt. 12
8 Gen. 16-17; Ps. 8; Matt. 13
9 Gen. 18-19; Ps. 9; Matt. 14-15
10 Gen. 20-21; Ps. 10; Matt. 16-17
11 Gen. 22-23; Ps. 11; Matt. 18
12 Gen. 24; Ps. 12; Matt. 19-20
13 Gen. 25-26; Ps. 13; Matt. 21
14 Gen. 27-28; Ps. 14; Matt. 22
15 Gen. 29-30; Ps. 15; Matt. 23
16 Gen. 31-32; Ps. 16; Matt. 24
17 Gen. 33-34; Ps. 17; Matt. 25
18 Gen. 35-36; Ps. 18; Matt. 26
19 Gen. 37-38; Ps. 19; Matt. 27
20 Gen. 39-40; Ps. 20; Matt. 28
21 Gen. 41-42; Ps. 21; Mark 1
22 Gen. 43-44; Ps. 22; Mark 2
23 Gen. 45-46; Ps. 23; Mark 3
24 Gen. 47-48; Ps. 24; Mark 4
25 Gen. 49-50; Ps. 25; Mark 5
26 Ex. 1-2; Ps. 26; Mark 6
27 Ex. 3-4; Ps. 27; Mark 7
28 Ex. 5-6; Ps. 28; Mark 8
29 Ex. 7-8; Ps. 29; Mark 9
30 Ex. 9-10; Ps. 30; Mark 10
31 Ex. 11-12; Ps. 31; Mark 11

FEBRUARY

1 Ex. 13-14; Ps. 32; Mark 12
2 Ex. 15-16; Ps. 33; Mark 13
3 Ex. 17-18; Ps. 34; Mark 14
4 Ex. 19-20; Ps. 35; Mark 15
5 Ex. 21-22; Ps. 36; Mark 16
6 Ex. 23-24; Ps. 37; Luke 1
7 Ex. 25-26; Ps. 38; Luke 2
8 Ex. 27-28; Ps. 39; Luke 3
9 Ex. 29-30; Ps. 40; Luke 4
10 Ex. 31-32; Ps. 41; Luke 5
11 Ex. 33-34; Ps. 42; Luke 6
12 Ex. 35-36; Ps. 43; Luke 7
13 Ex. 37-38; Ps. 44; Luke 8
14 Ex. 39-40; Ps. 45; Luke 9
15 Lev. 1-2; Ps. 46; Luke 10
16 Lev. 3-4; Ps. 47; Luke 11
17 Lev. 5-6; Ps. 48; Luke 12
18 Lev. 7-8; Ps. 49; Luke 13
19 Lev. 9-10; Ps. 50; Luke 14
20 Lev. 11-12; Ps. 51; Luke 15
21 Lev. 13; Ps. 52; Luke 16
22 Lev. 14; Ps. 53; Luke 17
23 Lev. 15-16; Ps. 54; Luke 18
24 Lev. 17-18; Ps. 55; Luke 19
25 Lev. 19-20; Ps. 56; Luke 20
26 Lev. 21-22; Ps. 57; Luke 21
27 Lev. 23-24; Ps. 58; Luke 22
28 Lev. 25
29 Ps. 59; Luke 23

MARCH

1 Lev. 26-27; Ps. 60; Luke 24
2 Num. 1-2; Ps. 61; John 1
3 Num. 3-4; Ps. 62; John 2-3
4 Num. 5-6; Ps. 63; John 4
5 Num. 7; Ps. 64; John 5
6 Num. 8-9; Ps. 65; John 6
7 Num. 10-11; Ps. 66; John 7
8 Num. 12-13; Ps. 67; John 8
9 Num. 14-15; Ps. 68; John 9
10 Num. 16; Ps. 69; John 10
11 Num. 17-18; Ps. 70; John 11
12 Num. 19-20; Ps. 71; John 12
13 Num. 21-22; Ps. 72; John 13
14 Num. 23-24; Ps. 73; John 14-15
15 Num. 25-26; Ps. 74; John 16
16 Num. 27-28; Ps. 75; John 17
17 Num. 29-30; Ps. 76; John 18
18 Num. 31-32; Ps. 77; John 19
19 Num. 33-34; Ps. 78; John 20
20 Num. 35-36; Ps. 79; John 21
21 Deut. 1-2; Ps. 80; Acts 1
22 Deut. 3-4; Ps. 81; Acts 2
23 Deut. 5-6; Ps. 82; Acts 3-4
24 Deut. 7-8; Ps. 83; Acts 5-6
25 Deut. 9-10; Ps. 84; Acts 7
26 Deut. 11-12; Ps. 85; Acts 8
27 Deut. 13-14; Ps. 86; Acts 9
28 Deut. 15-16; Ps. 87; Acts 10
29 Deut. 17-18; Ps. 88; Acts 11-12
30 Deut. 19-20; Ps. 89; Acts 13
31 Deut. 21-22; Ps. 90; Acts 14

APRIL

1 Deut. 23-24; Ps. 91; Acts 15
2 Deut. 25-27; Ps. 92; Acts 16
3 Deut. 28-29; Ps. 93; Acts 17
4 Deut. 30-31; Ps. 94; Acts 18
5 Deut. 32; Ps. 95; Acts 19
6 Deut. 33-34; Ps. 96; Acts 20
7 Josh. 1-2; Ps. 97; Acts 21
8 Josh. 3-4; Ps. 98; Acts 22
9 Josh. 5-6; Ps. 99; Acts 23
10 Josh. 7-8; Ps. 100; Acts 24-25
11 Josh. 9-10; Ps. 101; Acts 26
12 Josh. 11-12; Ps. 102; Acts 27
13 Josh. 13-14; Ps. 103; Acts 28
14 Josh. 15-16; Ps. 104; Rom. 1-2
15 Josh. 17-18; Ps. 105; Rom. 3-4
16 Josh. 19-20; Ps. 106; Rom. 5-6
17 Josh. 21-22; Ps. 107; Rom. 7-8
18 Josh. 23-24; Ps. 108; Rom. 9-10
19 Judg. 1-2; Ps. 109; Rom. 11-12
20 Judg. 3-4; Ps. 110; Rom. 13-14
21 Judg. 5-6; Ps. 111; Rom. 15-16
22 Judg. 7-8; Ps. 112; 1 Cor. 1-2
23 Judg. 9; Ps. 113; 1 Cor. 3-4
24 Judg. 10-11; Ps. 114; 1 Cor. 5-6
25 Judg. 12-13; Ps. 115; 1 Cor. 7
26 Judg. 14-15; Ps. 116; 1 Cor. 8-9
27 Judg. 16-17; Ps. 117; 1 Cor. 10
28 Judg. 18-19; Ps. 118; 1 Cor. 11
29 Judg. 20-21; Ps. 119:1-88; 1 Cor. 12
30 Ruth 1-4; Ps. 119:89-176; 1 Cor. 13

MAY

1 1 Sam. 1-2; Ps. 120; 1 Cor. 14
2 1 Sam. 3-4; Ps. 121; 1 Cor. 15
3 1 Sam. 5-6; Ps. 122; 1 Cor. 16
4 1 Sam. 7-8; Ps. 123; 2 Cor. 1
5 1 Sam. 9-10; Ps. 124; 2 Cor. 2-3
6 1 Sam. 11-12; Ps. 125; 2 Cor. 4-5
7 1 Sam. 13-14; Ps. 126; 2 Cor. 6-7
8 1 Sam. 15-16; Ps. 127; 2 Cor. 8
9 1 Sam. 17; Ps. 128; 2 Cor. 9-10
10 1 Sam. 18-19; Ps. 129; 2 Cor. 11
11 1 Sam. 20-21; Ps. 130; 2 Cor. 12
12 1 Sam. 22-23; Ps. 131; 2 Cor. 13
13 1 Sam. 24-25; Ps. 132; Gal. 1-2
14 1 Sam. 26-27; Ps. 133; Gal. 3-4
15 1 Sam. 28-29; Ps. 134; Gal. 5-6
16 1 Sam. 30-31; Ps. 135; Eph. 1-2
17 2 Sam. 1-2; Ps. 136; Eph. 3-4
18 2 Sam. 3-4; Ps. 137; Eph. 5-6
19 2 Sam. 5-6; Ps. 138; Phil. 1-2
20 2 Sam. 7-8; Ps. 139; Phil. 3-4
21 2 Sam. 9-10; Ps. 140; Col. 1-2
22 2 Sam. 11-12; Ps. 141; Col. 3-4
23 2 Sam. 13-14; Ps. 142; 1 Thess. 1-2
24 1 Sam. 15-16; Ps. 143; 1 Thess. 3-4
25 2 Sam. 17-18; Ps. 144; 1 Thess. 5
26 2 Sam. 19; Ps. 145; 2 Thess. 1-3
27 2 Sam. 20-21; Ps. 146; 1 Tim. 1-2
28 2 Sam. 22; Ps. 147; 1 Tim. 3-4
29 2 Sam. 23-24; Ps. 148; 1 Tim. 5-6
30 1 Kings 1; Ps. 149; 2 Tim. 1-2
31 1 Kings 2-3; Ps. 150; 2 Tim. 3-4

JUNE

1. 1 Kings 4-5; Prov. 1; Titus 1-3
2. 1 Kings 6-7; Prov. 2; Philem.
3. 1 Kings 8; Prov. 3; Heb. 1-2
4. 1 Kings 9-10; Prov. 4; Heb. 3-4
5. 1 Kings 11-12; Prov. 5; Heb. 5-6
6. 1 Kings 13-14; Prov. 6; Heb. 7-8
7. 1 Kings 15-16; Prov. 7; Heb. 9-10
8. 1 Kings 17-18; Prov. 8; Heb. 11
9. 1 Kings 19-20; Prov. 9; Heb. 12
10. 1 Kings 21-22; Prov. 10; Heb. 13
11. 2 Kings 1-2; Prov. 11; James 1
12. 2 Kings 3-4; Prov. 12; James 2-3
13. 2 Kings 5-6; Prov. 13; James 4-5
14. 2 Kings 7-8; Prov. 14; 1 Pet. 1
15. 2 Kings 9-10; Prov. 15; 1 Pet. 2-3
16. 2 Kings 11-12; Prov. 16; 1 Pet. 4-5
17. 2 Kings 13-14; Prov. 17; 2 Pet. 1-3
18. 2 Kings 15-16; Prov. 18; 1 John 1-2
19. 2 Kings 17; Prov. 19; 1 John 3-4
20. 2 Kings 18-19; Prov. 20; 1 John 5
21. 2 Kings 20-21; Prov. 21; 2 John
22. 2 Kings 22-23; Prov. 22; 3 John
23. 2 Kings 24-25; Prov. 23; Jude
24. 1 Chron. 1; Prov. 24; Rev. 1-2
25. 1 Chron. 2-3; Prov. 25; Rev. 3-5
26. 1 Chron. 4-5; Prov. 26; Rev. 6-7
27. 1 Chron. 6-7; Prov. 27; Rev. 8-10
28. 1 Chron. 8-9; Prov. 28; Rev. 11-12
29. 1 Chron. 10-11; Prov. 29; Rev. 13-14
30. 1 Chron. 12-13; Prov. 30; Rev. 15-17

JULY

1. 1 Chron. 14-15; Prov. 31; Rev. 18-19
2. 1 Chron. 16-17; Ps. 1; Rev. 20-22
3. 1 Chron. 18-19; Ps. 2; Matt. 1-2
4. 1 Chron. 20-21; Ps. 3; Matt. 3-4
5. 1 Chron. 22-23; Ps. 4; Matt. 5
6. 1 Chron. 24-25; Ps. 5; Matt. 6-7
7. 1 Chron. 26-27; Ps. 6; Matt. 8-9
8. 1 Chron. 28-29; Ps. 7; Matt. 10-11
9. 2 Chron. 1-2; Ps. 8; Matt. 12
10. 2 Chron. 3-4; Ps. 9; Matt. 13
11. 2 Chron. 5-6; Ps. 10; Matt. 14-15
12. 2 Chron. 7-8; Ps. 11; Matt. 16-17
13. 2 Chron. 9-10; Ps. 12; Matt. 18
14. 2 Chron. 11-12; Ps. 13; Matt. 19-20
15. 2 Chron. 13-14; Ps. 14; Matt. 21
16. 2 Chron. 15-16; Ps. 15; Matt. 22
17. 2 Chron. 17-18; Ps. 16; Matt. 23
18. 2 Chron. 19-20; Ps. 17; Matt. 24
19. 2 Chron. 21-22; Ps. 18; Matt. 25
20. 2 Chron. 23-24; Ps. 19; Matt. 26
21. 2 Chron. 25-26; Ps. 20; Matt. 27
22. 2 Chron. 27-28; Ps. 21; Matt. 28
23. 2 Chron. 29-30; Ps. 22; Mark 1
24. 2 Chron. 31-32; Ps. 23; Mark 2
25. 2 Chron. 33-34; Ps. 24; Mark 3
26. 2 Chron. 35-36; Ps. 25; Mark 4
27. Ezra 1-2; Ps. 26; Mark 5
28. Ezra 3-4; Ps. 27; Mark 6
29. Ezra 5-6; Ps. 28; Mark 7
30. Ezra 7-8; Ps. 29; Mark 8
31. Ezra 9-10; Ps. 30; Mark 9

AUGUST

1 Neh. 1-2; Ps. 31; Mark 10
2 Neh. 3-4; Ps. 32; Mark 11
3 Neh. 5-6; Ps. 33; Mark 12
4 Neh. 7; Ps. 34; Mark 13
5 Neh. 8-9; Ps. 35; Mark 14
6 Neh. 10-11; Ps. 36; Mark 15
7 Neh. 12-13; Ps. 37; Mark 16
8 Esth. 1-2; Ps. 38; Luke 1
9 Esth. 3-4; Ps. 39; Luke 2
10 Esth. 5-6; Ps. 40; Luke 3
11 Esth. 7-8; Ps. 41; Luke 4
12 Esth. 9-10; Ps. 42; Luke 5
13 Job 1-2; Ps. 43; Luke 6
14 Job 3-4; Ps. 44; Luke 7
15 Job 5-6; Ps. 45; Luke 8
16 Job 7-8; Ps. 46; Luke 9
17 Job 9-10; Ps. 47; Luke 10
18 Job 11-12; Ps. 48; Luke 11
19 Job 13-14; Ps. 49; Luke 12
20 Job 15-16; Ps. 50; Luke 13
21 Job 17-18; Ps. 51; Luke 14
22 Job 19-20; Ps. 52; Luke 15
23 Job 21-22; Ps. 53; Luke 16
24 Job 23-25; Ps. 54; Luke 17
25 Job 26-28; Ps. 55; Luke 18
26 Job 29-30; Ps. 56; Luke 19
27 Job 31-32; Ps. 57; Luke 20
28 Job 33-34; Ps. 58; Luke 21
29 Job 35-36; Ps. 59; Luke 22
30 Job 37-38; Ps. 60; Luke 23
31 Job 39-40; Ps. 61; Luke 24

SEPTEMBER

1 Job 41-42; Ps. 62; John 1
2 Eccl. 1-2; Ps. 63; John 2-3
3 Eccl. 3-4; Ps. 64; John 4
4 Eccl. 5-6; Ps. 65; John 5
5 Eccl. 7-8; Ps. 66; John 6
6 Eccl. 9-10; Ps. 67; John 7
7 Eccl. 11-12; Ps. 68; John 8
8 Song of Sol. 1-2; Ps. 69; John 9
9 Song of Sol. 3-4; Ps. 70; John 10
10 Song of Sol. 5-6; Ps. 71; John 11
11 Song of Sol. 7-8; Ps. 72; John 12
12 Isaiah 1-2; Ps. 73; John 13
13 Isaiah 3-5; Ps. 74; John 14-15
14 Isaiah 6-8; Ps. 75; John 16
15 Isaiah 9-10; Ps. 76; John 17
16 Isaiah 11-13; Ps. 77; John 18
17 Isaiah 14-15; Ps. 78; John 19
18 Isaiah 16-17; Ps. 79; John 20
19 Isaiah 18-19; Ps. 80; John 21
20 Isaiah 20-22; Ps. 81; Acts 1
21 Isaiah 23-24; Ps. 82; Acts 2
22 Isaiah 25-26; Ps. 83; Acts 3-4
23 Isaiah 27-28; Ps. 84; Acts 5-6
24 Isaiah 29-30; Ps. 85; Acts 7
25 Isaiah 31-32; Ps. 86; Acts 8
26 Isaiah 33-34; Ps. 87; Acts 9
27 Isaiah 35-36; Ps. 88; Acts 10
28 Isaiah 37-38; Ps. 89; Acts 11-12
29 Isaiah 39-40; Ps. 90; Acts 13
30 Isaiah 41-42; Ps. 91; Acts 14

OCTOBER

1 Isaiah 43-44; Ps. 92; Acts 15
2 Isaiah 45-46; Ps. 93; Acts 16
3 Isaiah 47-48; Ps. 94; Acts 17
4 Isaiah 49-50; Ps. 95; Acts 18
5 Isaiah 51-52; Ps. 96; Acts 19
6 Isaiah 53-54; Ps. 97; Acts 20
7 Isaiah 55-56; Ps. 98; Acts 21
8 Isaiah 57-58; Ps. 99; Acts 22
9 Isaiah 59-60; Ps. 100; Acts 23
10 Isaiah 61-62; Ps. 101; Acts 24-25
11 Isaiah 63-64; Ps. 102; Acts 26
12 Isaiah 65-66; Ps. 103; Acts 27
13 Jer. 1-2; Ps. 104; Acts 28
14 Jer. 3-4; Ps. 105; Rom. 1-2
15 Jer. 5-6; Ps. 106; Rom. 3-4
16 Jer. 7-8; Ps. 107; Rom. 5-6
17 Jer. 9-10; Ps. 108; Rom. 7-8
18 Jer. 11-12; Ps. 109; Rom. 9-10
19 Jer. 13-14; Ps. 110; Rom. 11-12
20 Jer. 15-16; Ps. 111; Rom. 13-14
21 Jer. 17-18; Ps. 112; Rom. 15-16
22 Jer. 19-20; Ps. 113; 1 Cor. 1-2
23 Jer. 21-22; Ps. 114; 1 Cor. 3-4
24 Jer. 23-24; Ps. 115; 1 Cor. 5-6
25 Jer. 25-26; Ps. 116; 1 Cor. 7
26 Jer. 27-28; Ps. 117; 1 Cor. 8-9
27 Jer. 29-30; Ps. 118; 1 Cor. 10
28 Jer. 31-32; Ps. 119:1-64; 1 Cor. 11
29 Jer. 33-34; Ps. 119:65-120; 1 Cor. 12
30 Jer. 35-36; Ps. 119:121-176; 1 Cor. 13
31 Jer. 37-38; Ps. 120; 1 Cor. 14

NOVEMBER

1 Jer. 39-40; Ps. 121; 1 Cor. 15
2 Jer. 41-42; Ps. 122; 1 Cor. 16
3 Jer. 43-44; Ps. 123; 2 Cor. 1
4 Jer. 45-46; Ps. 124; 2 Cor. 2-3
5 Jer. 47-48; Ps. 125; 2 Cor. 4-5
6 Jer. 49-50; Ps. 126; 2 Cor. 6-7
7 Jer. 51-52; Ps. 127; 2 Cor. 8
8 Lam. 1-2; Ps. 128; 2 Cor. 9-10
9 Lam. 3; Ps. 129; 2 Cor. 11
10 Lam. 4-5; Ps. 130; 2 Cor. 12
11 Ezek. 1-2; Ps. 131; 2 Cor. 13
12 Ezek. 3-4; Ps. 132; Gal. 1-2
13 Ezek. 5-6; Ps. 133; Gal. 3-4
14 Ezek. 7-8; Ps. 134; Gal. 5-6
15 Ezek. 9-10; Ps. 135; Eph. 1-2
16 Ezek. 11-12; Ps. 136; Eph. 3-4
17 Ezek. 13-14; Ps. 137; Eph. 5-6
18 Ezek. 15-16; Ps. 138; Phil. 1-2
19 Ezek. 17-18; Ps. 139; Phil. 3-4
20 Ezek. 19-20; Ps. 140; Col. 1-2
21 Ezek. 21-22; Ps. 141; Col. 3-4
22 Ezek. 23-24; Ps. 142; 1 Thess. 1-2
23 Ezek. 25-26; Ps. 143; 1 Thess. 3-4
24 Ezek. 27-28; Ps. 144; 1 Thess. 5
25 Ezek. 29-30; Ps. 145; 2 Thess. 1-3
26 Ezek. 31-32; Ps. 146; 1 Tim. 1-2
27 Ezek. 33-34; Ps. 147; 1 Tim. 3-4
28 Ezek. 35-36; Ps. 148; 1 Tim. 5-6
29 Ezek. 37-38; Ps. 149; 2 Tim. 1-2
30 Ezek. 39-40; Ps. 150; 2 Tim. 3-4

DECEMBER

1 Ezek. 41-42; Prov. 1; Titus 1-3
2 Ezek. 43-44; Prov. 2; Philem.
3 Ezek. 45-46; Prov. 3; Heb. 1-2
4 Ezek. 47-48; Prov. 4; Heb. 3-4
5 Dan. 1-2; Prov. 5; Heb. 5-6
6 Dan. 3-4; Prov. 6; Heb. 7-8
7 Dan. 5-6; Prov. 7; Heb. 9-10
8 Dan. 7-8; Prov. 8; Heb. 11
9 Dan. 9-10; Prov. 9; Heb. 12
10 Dan. 11-12; Prov. 10; Heb. 13
11 Hos. 1-3; Prov. 11; James 1-3
12 Hos. 4-6; Prov. 12; James 4-5
13 Hos. 7-8; Prov. 13; 1 Pet. 1
14 Hos. 9-11; Prov. 14; 1 Pet. 2-3
15 Hos. 12-14; Prov. 15; 1 Pet. 4-5
16 Joel 1-3; Prov. 16; 2 Pet. 1-3
17 Amos 1-3; Prov. 17; 1 John 1-2
18 Amos 4-6; Prov. 18; 1 John 3-4
19 Amos 7-9; Prov. 19; 1 John 5
20 Obad.; Prov. 20; 2 John
21 Jonah 1-4; Prov. 21; 3 John
22 Mic. 1-4; Prov. 22; Jude
23 Mic. 5-7; Prov. 23; Rev. 1-2
24 Nah. 1-3; Prov. 24; Rev. 3-5
25 Hab. 1-3; Prov. 25; Rev. 6-7
26 Zeph. 1-3; Prov. 26; Rev. 8-10
27 Hag. 1-2; Prov. 27; Rev. 11-12
28 Zech. 1-4; Prov. 28; Rev. 13-14
29 Zech. 5-9; Prov. 29; Rev. 15-17
30 Zech. 10-14; Prov. 30; Rev. 18-19
31 Mal. 1-4; Prov. 31; Rev. 20-22

Bibliography

Exley, Richard, *Building Relationships That Last — Life's Bottom Line.* Tulsa: Honor Books, 1990.

Mills, Dick. *A Word in Season, Vol. I.* Tulsa: Harrison House, 1986.

Word Ministries. *Prayers That Avail Much, Vol. I.* Tulsa: Harrison House, 1989.

Word Ministries. *Prayers That Avail Much, Vol. II.* Tulsa: Harrison House, 1989.

Write: Word Ministries • P. O. Box 76532 • Atlanta, GA 30358

Additional copies of this book are available
from your local bookstore or from:
Harrison House • P. O. Box 35035 • Tulsa, OK 74153

The Harrison House Vision

Proclaiming the truth and the power
Of the Gospel of Jesus Christ
With excellence;

Challenging Christians to
Live victoriously,
Grow spiritually,
Know God intimately.